LADDER TO HEAVEN

Mom's Everyday Prayers
for a Successful School Year

Wildine Pierre

To Chris and Angel: No matter how much I say I love you, I always love you more than that

To my mom, whose prayers made me who I am today

* * *

To all the moms too tired to pick up that cup of coffee, and too busy for self-care

May your prayers be heard
your hearts stay full
and your children forever grateful

LEAVE A ***** REVIEW

As an incentive for leaving a review, visit my website @ www.wildinepierre.com and sign up to be part of my fan club.

On the site you will find:

- Exclusive Q&A's with the author
- The books official page (lots of information)
- Several Giveaways
- Chance to win an AUTOGRAPHED+ PERSONALIZED paperback of my latest release

And follow me on:

- Facebook:https://www.facebook.com/wild.numa
- Twitter:https://twitter.com/WildLovesWords
- Instagram:https://www.instagram.-com/p/Cf4ZWw_pPSH/?igshid=YmMyMTA2M2Y=

- Goodreads:https://www.goodreads.com/author/dashboard?ref=nav_profile_authordash

You're the best!!

-Wildine

TABLE OF CONTENTS

INTRODUCTION

WHY DO WE PRAY?

As a new mom, I was intent on being the perfect Christian mom. I was teaching bible school and was the leader of children's church ministry, so I had particular ideas about what that meant.

Unfortunately, most of these ideas were wrong, and some came from imperfect people! I didn't pray about it. I didn't have time; I was frustrated from the sleepless nights and the many responsibilities of being everyone else rock but my own.

I went from book to group to message board to figure out the secrets to being that perfect mom. That motivation quickly became a nightmare when my children misbehaved at school and showed temper signs. They were being bullied by those who felt threatened by their innocence. I needed to seek guidance, and I needed to pray. So I did just that before sending them to school; Hallelujah, for the power of prayer.

Prayers before school and thorough the day allow us to realize our dependence on God's strength over our own. The life we live is our most incredible testimony. And perhaps the most important audience is our children. You have to believe that your children have been set apart to serve God, that they will walk with God, love God, serve God, and please God!

But why are we praying? We're praying against a hostile culture I never thought I would see in my lifetime. We are praying for children to come to know Jesus, stand boldly in their faith, and provide support and encouragement to moms carrying heavy burdens for their children. We are praying for schools to be directed by biblical values and high moral standards. We are praying for the opportunity, to witness God bring revival and spiritual awakening to many who are fearful and walking in darkness.

May this devotional help you steer your children back to God to discover how to train them in God's way. May your children ultimately trust God, so they may hear His voice above all others and find their purpose and passions early in life. Make these devotions a part of your daily life, and watch the benefits as your children walk the path of truth, holiness, and success!

RAISING GODLY KIDS

SCRIPTURE 1

SCRIPTURE: (Proverbs 22:6 KJV)

Train up a child in the way he should go: and when he is old, he will not depart from it.

DEEPER REFLECTION

Train a child in the way he should go as Abraham trained his children, and those born in his house, in the way of the Lord and in the way of justice and judgment. What are the ways in which they should go, and what will be the benefits and advantages? Read **(Genesis 14:14 KJV)**. It is the duty of parents and teachers in all ages, and under the present gospel dispensation, to bring those under their care into the nurture and admonition of the Lord **(Ephesians 6:4 KJV)**, and when they are old, they will not go away; not easily or ordinarily.

There are exceptions to this observation; but in general, when there is a good education, the impressions of it do not wear out easily, and as they reach years of maturity and understanding, their hearts are seasoned with the grace of God, and they are enabled to put into practice what they learned in theory, and so they continue in the paths of truth and holiness.

PRAYER

Father God, you set the example of how to love others and teach your words by sending Jesus to the earth. Help me to train and instruct my own children and everyone who looks up to me in the same way. Let my actions and words be the wisdom that teaches others. I pray that my children will live a life worthy of you, please you in every way, bearing fruit while doing good work and growing in your knowledge, AMEN.

TEACHING KIDS TO PRAY

SCRIPTURE 2

SCRIPTURE: (Deuteronomy 11:19 NKJV)

You shall teach them to your children, speaking of them when you sit in your house, when you walk by the way, when you lie down, and when you rise up.

DEEPER REFLECTION

God longs for us to know and love him from our childhood. Parents are responsible for teaching our children to love God with all their hearts, with all their souls, and with all their strength. This is best done by example. If they see that our love for God and the desire to please Him are the basis of our actions, they will learn to live a life that glorifies God.

We should also read and memorize the word of God as a family. In the Bible, we find words of life that teach us what pleases God and transforms us. As we grow, we face new challenges. If in those moments, we remember a Bible verse learned during childhood, we will instantly receive the necessary word of wisdom, encouragement, or healing. **(Deuteronomy 6:5-7 NKJV)**

PRAYER

Heavenly Father, keep me alert to the dangers of falling into a worldly mindset and help me to keep the eyes of my heart on Jesus. Help me to teach the truth of God's Word to my children at every opportunity and protect the hearts and minds of my children . This I pray in Jesus' name, AMEN.

CHILDREN IN THE BIBLE

SCRIPTURE 3

SCRIPTURE: (Psalm 127:3 NKJV)

Behold, children are a heritage from the LORD, The fruit of the womb is a reward.

DEEPER REFLECTION

'Behold, children are an inheritance from the Lord'. Solomon was sensitive to this. Especially, if by sons he meant good sons, as in **Proverbs 18:22**, by wife he meant a good wife. A poor man who does not have an inheritance in any other way has one from the Lord because such are often full of children; neither can he wish, as a graceless man did, that God would keep those blessings to himself, because he had too many.

It's your reward. That is, your free gift; and God will be his great reward if, through the prayer and good education of his parents, they turn out benevolent, as an inheritance from the Lord, and as arrows in your hand.

PRAYER

Lord, I pray my children would love you with their heart, soul, and mind, and I pray they would believe the truth about who they are in Christ. Lord give our children a strong desire for your Word. May they have a hunger for more of You and may they find your Word sweeter than honey, AMEN.

GOD'S PLAN OF SALVATION

SCRIPTURE 4

SCRIPTURE: (1 John 3:2 NKJV)

Beloved, now we are children of God; and it has not yet been revealed what we shall be, but we know that when He is revealed, we shall be like Him, for we shall see Him as He is.

DEEPER REFLECTION

Now we are the children of God. Yes! For though we carry with us a body of sin and death, as we do, yet by regeneration, being quickened in our spiritual part, we are made partakers of the divine nature, having escaped the corruption that is in the world by regeneration. **2 Peter 1:4**.

Therefore, we are now, to all intents and purposes, children of God. But of the glory, yes, that eternal glory, to which we are begotten and called by Christ Jesus, there are no images or likenesses that we are familiar with here below, by which we can explain it. Moreover, the eye has not seen, nor ear heard, nor has it entered the hearts of men to conceive, the nature or extent of that glory that will be revealed.

But this we know, that in the midst of all that lack of

conformity that we now have with the person and image of our Lord, there will then be a resemblance, because we will see him as He is. **2 Corinthians 3:18.**

PRAYER

Lord Jesus, I pray that you cleanse my children of all my iniquity and unrighteousness. Father, make their hearts soft to the penetrating truth of your word, sow your truths deeply and eternally in them. Father, may my children know this incomprehensible love and be moved with love for you. Please send your Holy Spirit to help them obey you and to do your will for the rest of their lives. In Jesus' name I pray, AMEN.

TEACHING GOD'S WORD

SCRIPTURE 5

SCRIPTURE: (Colossians 3:16 NKJV)

Let the word of Christ dwell in you richly in all wisdom, teaching and admonishing one another in psalms and hymns and spiritual songs, singing with grace in your hearts to the Lord.

DEEPER REFLECTION

Let the word of Christ - The doctrine of Christ, Dwell in you richly in all wisdom - Abundantly, producing the spirit of true wisdom. That doctrine is adapted to make you wise. This means that you should deposit the doctrines of the gospel in your hearts and in your children's heart and meditate on them; to allow them to be your guide, and to lovingly improve you for the best purpose.

Teaching and admonition; **Ephesians 5:19-20**. The only additional thought here is that his psalms and hymns were to be regarded as a method of "teaching" and "admonition"; that is, they must be imbued with truth and be such as to lift the mind away from error and sin. It is true in a more important sense that he who is allowed to make the hymns of a church needs little care of who preaches or who makes the creed. He will more effectually shape the sentiments of a church than those who preach or make creeds and confessions. Therefore, it is indispensable to preserve the truth that the sacred songs of a church should be imbued with a solid evangelical sentiment.

PRAYER

Heavenly Father, give us faith to receive your word, understanding to know what it means, and the will to put it into practice especially in our children's lives; Lord, I pray my children would believe in you with a devoted heart as I teach them Your Word, help them to never depart from it, through Jesus Christ our Lord, AMEN.

FOOLISHNESS

SCRIPTURE 6

SCRIPTURE: (Proverbs 18:2-3 NKJV)

A fool has no delight in understanding, But in expressing his own heart. When the wicked cometh, then cometh also contempt, and with ignominy reproach.

DEEPER REFLECTION

The fool does not like intelligence, but that his heart discovers itself. Or, in discovering his own heart, that is, in following his own humor, against everything that can be said to be contrary. He is willful and therefore stands like a stake in the middle of a stream; He lets everyone walk past him, but he is where he was. It is easier to deal with the reasons of twenty men than with the will of one man. **Proverbs 1:7, 22.**

If he has reached his conclusion, you can remove a stone as soon as he does. His will is his rule. Some think that Solomon here taxes, not so much obstinacy, as the vain glory and ostentation of affectionate fools, who seem to delight in wisdom; but it is only for a name, and so that, by putting their good parts in the sun, they may win the applause and admiration of the world, by singularly qualified men. **Proverbs 17:16.**

PRAYER

Lord Jesus, forgive me that sometimes, in foolishness, I still try to do things my own way. Direct me to have complete dependence on you so I can direct my children each day for your guidance. May my children not walk in blindness to the ways of the wicked. Open their eyes to see clearly where foolishness leads. Grant them discernment to recognize the tricks of the enemy. May the taste of foolishness in their mouths be bitter and unsatisfying, leaving them with an insatiable thirst for Wisdom instead. In Jesus's Name I pray, Amen.

JEALOUSY

SCRIPTURE 7

SCRIPTURE: (Proverbs 27:4 NKJV)

Wrath is cruel and anger a torrent, but who is able to stand before jealousy?

DEEPER REFLECTION

Anger is cruel, and anger is scandalous; but who is capable of stopping before envy?

Envy is a snake in the grass. Christians, beware of envy. Perhaps you will be tempted to hold him in your heart when you see another Christian more useful than you, or when a Christian brother seems to have more honor than you. Oh so! Cry to God against it. Never let this poisonous reptile be spared for a single moment. The best of men will find envy creeping over them at times; it may be the envy of the wicked who are rich. We must try to overcome that at once. And even the envy of the best of men is covetousness and hatred, a violation of two commandments. God save us from that!

PRAYER

Lord Jesus, give my children the desire to become Holy like you. Set them free from anxious thoughts that cause them to become jealous of others, free my children from jealousy Lord. Uproot jealousy from my children's heart that they may stop acting like a mere human. Help them to behave like children of God that is born of the spirit. Please teach them how to be appreciative of others even when it is hard. In Jesus' name, I believe and pray, AMEN.

PERSISTENCE

SCRIPTURE 8

SCRIPTURE: (Ephesians 6:18 NKJV)

Praying always with all prayer and supplication in the Spirit, being watchful to this end with all perseverance and supplication for all the saints.

DEEPER REFLECTION

It would be good for the soldier who goes out into battle to pray, to pray for victory; or pray that he be prepared for death, should he fall. But soldiers don't usually feel the need for this. For the Christian soldier, however, it is indispensable. Prayer crowns all legal efforts with success and gives a victory when nothing else would. It doesn't matter how complete the armor is; no matter how skilled we may be in the science of warfare; No matter how brave we are, we can be sure that without prayer, we will be defeated. Only God can give victory; and when the Christian soldier goes out fully armed for spiritual conflict, if he looks to God in prayer, he can be sure of a triumph. This prayer should not be intermittent. It is always to be regular. In every temptation and spiritual conflict, we must pray. **LUKE 18:1**

Therefore, Christians who believe in God must be persistent in praying; otherwise, they might fall back. **Matthew 6:6.**

PRAYER

Help my children and I Lord to stand; give us the strength and courage to be persistent in prayer. If we desire good things, remind us that we need to pray and pray again. In Jesus' name we pray, AMEN.

ANGER

SCRIPTURE 9

ANGER

SCRIPTURE: (Ecclesiastes 7:9 NKJV)

Do not hasten in your spirit to be angry, for anger rests in the bosom of fools.

DEEPER REFLECTION

Do not rush in your spirit to be angry. The hasty man, we say, never wants affliction. Because anger is a bad adviser, and it involves a man in many anguishes, evils, and misfortunes. He makes a man like a bee, that vengeful creature that, in revenge, loses its sting and becomes a drone; or, like Tamar, who, to be on a par with her mother-in-law, defiled herself with incest. James 1:19.

Because anger rests in the bosom of fools. A fool may rush into the bosom of a sage, but he will not rest there or dwell there; he only dwells where he rule, and only where a fool is the master of the family. Thunder, hail, tempest, no nuisance or damage to heavenly bodies. He sees to it that the sun does not go down on this wicked guest; try that the soul does not crack or become impure with it, because anger corrupts the heart, like yeast in dough, or vinegar in the vessel in which it remains. Proverbs 14:29

PRAYER

Everlasting God, your peace surpasses all my understanding. When anger rises within us, please calm my mind and soothe our hearts with your gentle words. Look upon us and cause your face to shine upon us. Father, I lift my children to You asking that You inhabit their emotions. Surround them with Your love so they may be encouraged and strengthened in how they manage and express their feelings in healthy ways. Do not let them be controlled by fits of rage, revenge, jealousy, or malicious words and actions. Instead, give them wisdom and understanding, inclining them toward a gentle and thoughtful spirit.Through Jesus Christ, our Lord, AMEN.

STRESS

SCRIPTURE 10

SCRIPTURE: (Isaiah 41:10 NKJV)

Fear not, for I am with you; be not dismayed, for I am your God. I will strengthen you, Yes, I will help you, and I will uphold you with my righteous right hand.

DEEPER REFLECTION

God speaks tenderly; Do not fear, because I am with you: not only within the call, but present with you. Are you weak? I will strengthen you. Do you need friends? I will help you in your time of need. Are you ready to fall? I will hold you with that right hand that is full of justice, doling out rewards and punishments. There are those who fight with the people of God, who seek their ruin. The people of God do not do evil for evil, but wait for God's time. It is the Jacob worm; so little, so weak, so despised and trampled by everybody. The people of God are like worms, in humble thoughts of themselves and in the haughty thoughts of their enemies; worms, but not vipers, not from the seed of the serpent. **Deuteronomy 20:1, Romans 8:31**

PRAYER

Dear God, I come before you to lay any panic and stress and anxiety that we may have at your feet. When we are crushed by our fears and worries, remind us of your power and your grace. Fill us with your peace as we trust in you and you alone. For this, we thank you, AMEN.

CALL TO BE DIFFERENT

SCRIPTURE 11

SCRIPTURE: (Romans 12:6 NKJV)

Having then gifts differing according to the grace that is given to us, let us use them: if prophecy, let us prophesy in proportion to our faith.

DEEPER REFLECTION

Having then gifts, differing, ... as in a natural body, the various members of it do not have the same office, and do not perform the same actions, so they do not have the same faculties, but different faculties; Thus, in the spiritual body, the Church, since there are different members, these members do not have the same work and the businesses assigned to some are used in one way, and some others; They also have diversities of gifts for their different administrations and operations, and all from Christ their head, for the same spirit, and for the service of the whole body. **(1 Corinthians 7:7)**

According to the grace that he gives us; Because all these gifts are not the effects of nature, the fruits of human power, diligence, and industry, but flow from the grace of God, who presents them when, where, and to whom He please in a free and sovereign way; and therefore to be recognized as such, and accustomed to His glory, and for the good of His church and His people. **(1 Corinthians 12:4)**

PRAYER

Heavenly Father, I know that we have been put on this earth for a greater purpose. You have called us to love you first and foremost, and you have also called us to love and serve our neighbors. As your hands and feet, help us to fulfill the primary calling of our being. Help my children to understand that they are fearfully and wonderfully made and are called to be different from others. May they bear the fruit of the Spirit and exhibit love, joy, peace, patience, kindness, goodness, faithfulness, gentleness and self-control in their daily walk. Help them to conduct themselves in a worthy manner that will please your heart, AMEN.

COMMITMENT TO CHRIST

SCRIPTURE 12

SCRIPTURE: (Deuteronomy 11:1 NKJV)

Therefore you shall love the LORD your God, and keep His charge, His statutes, His judgments, and His commandments always.

DEEPER REFLECTION

Therefore, you shall love the Lord your God. The whole discourse has this scope, that the people must testify their gratitude for their obedience, and thus be enticed by God's rewards, they must embrace his Law with reverence. Also, for this reason, he requires them to love God, before exhorting them to obey the Law itself. Because, although he could have ordered them imperiously and threateningly, he preferred to gently guide them to obedience, presenting before them the sweetness of his grace. In short, he exhorts them that, being invited by God's love, they should love him in return. In the meantime, it is well to note that free affection is the foundation and beginning of duly obeying the Law, since what arises from restraint or servile fear cannot please God. **(Deuteronomy 11:13, Zechariah 3:7).**

PRAYER

O Lord God, as we submit ourselves to you, we commit to doing everything we do, to saying everything we say, and to choosing everything we choose. May I never stop praying for this gift you've entrusted to me. Lord, let my commitment to raise my children for the glory of your name cause his life to forever testify of your faithfulness.We pray that they will not lean on their own understanding and comprise the truth of God's Word, for the sake of Your Kingdom and not ours, AMEN.

CONTENTMENT

SCRIPTURE 13

SCRIPTURE: (1 Timothy 6:6 NKJV)

Now godliness with contentment is great gain.

DEEPER REFLECTION

1 Timothy 6:6. But great gain is godliness accompanied by contentment... The word godliness, here, and in several other places in this epistle, means the true religion, Christianity; and the word contentment means a competence, a sufficiency; that measure or portion of secular things which is necessary for the sustenance of life, while the great work of regeneration is carried on in the soul. Not what this or that person may consider a competition, but what is necessary for the mere purposes of life in reference to the other world; food, clothing, and lodging. **1 Timothy 6:7.** Therefore, if a man has the life of God in his soul, and only a sufficiency of food and clothing to preserve and not burden life, he has what God calls great gain, an abundant portion.

PRAYER

Father, I give all praise and glory to your most holy name. Help me today as I Seek contentment in everything I do. Help my children to be grateful and content with what I provide as a mother. Help them to turn away from the comparison culture and striving for more by thanking the Lord for all of the blessings, AMEN.

JUDGEMENT

SCRIPTURE 14

SCRIPTURE: (Romans 14:13 NKJV)

Therefore let us not judge one another anymore, but rather resolve this, not to put a stumbling block or a cause to fall in our brother's way.

DEEPER REFLECTION

Romans 14:13. Therefore, let us no longer judge each other...Let us abandon such reckless conduct; it is dangerous, it is uncharitable: the judgment belongs to the Lord, and he will condemn only those who should not be acquitted.

Let no one lay a stumbling block... Let both Jew and Gentile converts consider that they should work to further each other's spiritual interests, and not be a means of hindering each other in their Christian course; or make them abandon the Gospel, because the salvation of their souls does not depend on questions of rites and ceremonies. **(Romans 14:4-10, James 4:11).**

PRAYER

Father, my spirit is willing, but my flesh is wounded and weak. Keep me in your hands, Father, and protect me from falling into the hands of my enemies. Give me good judgment, so I can help my children so they will not fall for the tricks of the Devil. I pray You will guard my children's mind from harmful instruction, and grant them discernment to recognize truth that can only be found in You. In Jesus Name, AMEN.

GUILT

SCRIPTURE 15

SCRIPTURE: (John 3:17 NKJV)

For God did not send His Son into the world to condemn the world, but that the world through Him might be saved.

DEEPER REFLECTION

We must have a new nature, new principles, new affections, and new goals. By our first birth, we were corrupt, formed in sin; therefore, we must be made new creatures. No stronger expression could have been chosen to signify a great and more remarkable change of state and character. We must be completely different from what we were before, since what begins to be at any moment is not and cannot be the same as what was before. This new birth is from heaven, John 1:13, and its tendency is towards the sky. It is a great change wrought in the heart of a sinner by the power of the Holy Spirit. It means that something is done in us, and by us, that we cannot do for ourselves. Something is wrong, for which such a life begins that will last forever. We cannot otherwise expect any benefit from Christ; it is necessary for our happiness here and in the future.

PRAYER

Forgive us, Lord. We have sinned today and need to ask for your forgiveness. Please take away our guilt and wipe our slate clean with the blood of Jesus Christ, of which we are so unworthy. Please forgive me for past wrongs concerning my children. Thank you for Your grace that covers all my sin and allows me the chance to start again. I understand that guilt is a condemning voice, and therefore it isn't from You. Lord, help me let go of things I cannot change and look instead to the blessings of today. In Jesus' name, AMEN.

INTEGRITY

SCRIPTURE 16

SCRIPTURE: (Proverbs 28:6 NKJV)

Better is the poor who walks in his integrity than one perverse in his ways, though he be rich.

DEEPER REFLECTION

There are times of difficult tests for the children of God. Sometimes the people we love can become the mouth of the enemy to question or ridicule our faith.

However, even if our friends and family cannot understand why God allows us to go through such situations, we must follow Job's example and maintain our integrity before Him. The Bible tells us that after Job had lost everything except his life, his friends came to visit and comfort him. But after expressing their condolences and mourning for his situation, these men turned into prosecutors, accusing him of having committed some hidden sin.

In their human logic, these three men thought that it was not possible that all these evils would come to Job if he had walked in integrity and obedience before God. His continual accusations led Job to defend his testimony with intensity to the end. **(Job 27:5 KJV)** God forbid that I should justify you: till I die I will not remove mine integrity from me.

PRAYER

Father, we ask that you make our paths forward and safe as we choose integrity. We also ask that you would shed light on those who follow crooked paths. May we see a new wave of integrity sweeping over our nation by the power of the Holy Spirit. In Jesus' Name, AMEN.

LAZINESS

SCRIPTURE 17

SCRIPTURE: (Proverbs 12:24 NKJV)

The hand of the diligent will rule, but the lazy man will be put to forced labor.

DEEPER REFLECTION

The hand of the diligent must carry the rule, "He will become rich", Through diligence, men obtain riches, and through riches, they come to power and authority over others: from apprentices and record workers, they become masters of their trade; Diligent men become masters of families and have servants and workers under them; they become magistrates in the cities, and perform through their fellow citizens, and are advanced to places of power and authority in the Commonwealth; **(Proverbs 22:29)**.

But the lazy must be under tribute; the "lazy hand" or "deceitful hand", by which it can be lent and supplied; Generally, for such who are lazy, and do not care about business, convinced of deceitful methods, cheating, and we share; and such being subject to others, to them that are diligent; hence it is said to be

"Under homage", or affluent; for those who are tributaries are in subjection to those to whom they pay tribute.

PRAYER

Father in heaven, I destroy every form of laziness that may reduce my productivity and every laziness at the edge of my breakthrough. I ask the same for my children, may they be productive like no other. May they always exhibit the fruits of the Spirit – love, joy, peace, patience, kindness, goodness, faithfulness, gentleness, and self-control. Let them be fountains of blessing to everyone around them, AMEN.

POPULARITY

SCRIPTURE 18

SCRIPTURE: (Proverbs 13:20 NKJV)

He who walks with wise men will be wise, but the companion of fools will be destroyed.

DEEPER REFLECTION

He who walks with wise men will be wise. Who is a companion of them that fear the Lord?; he frequently converses with them in private on spiritual and experiential things, and walks with them in public in all the commandments and ordinances of the Lord; By those means, he grows wiser and wiser, he gains a great stock of spiritual knowledge and experience; For this, he stands well in both natural and spiritual wisdom, a man of no ability will improve by keeping company wise.

But a fellow fool will be destroyed; The Latin version of the Vulgate is, "he shall become like them"; be dumb as they are, and grow even dumber and dumber. The Septuagint version is, "will be known"; known by the company that it is still a fool too: or rather, "it will break"; Ruined and destroyed, "Evil Communications Corrupt Good Manners", **1 Corinthians 15:33**, and thus bring ruin and destruction.

PRAYER

Give us the strength, we pray, to be willing to lose the crowd, to stand alone, to be despised for you. We know that being close to you might distance us from our friends. But we are willing to pay that price. I'm praying that my children would, by God's grace, find their worth and identity in Jesus rather than in the likes they receive from others. Help us Lord, AMEN.

PRIORITIES

SCRIPTURE 19

SCRIPTURE: (Colossians 3:2 NKJV)

Set your mind on things above, not on things on the earth.

DEEPER REFLECTION

Set your affections on the things above, so that unless the effects are fixed on them, they will never be properly sought after. The Word means a lot to those who care, and think of them, favor and approve of them, to be lovingly desirous, and concerned about them; For where is the treasure, the heart must be; and as the best things of saints are above, their minds and affections must be there in the same way; Your contemplation must be on those things, and your conversation must be in heaven; Nor should they consider anything, but what is there, or comes from there, because they do not belong to this world, but to another and better country: their citizenship is in heaven, and there, in a short time, they must have their eternal residence. Therefore, they must seek, and highly prize and value heavenly things, not things on earth.

Never mind the Earth and earthly things, temporary enjoyment, riches and honors; And though food and clothing, and the necessities of life, must be sought, and cared for, and provided for, but not with the anxiety and perplexity of mind, in a too thoughtful and anxious way; Neither should the heart be set on those outward things, or happiness placed in possession of them. **(1 Chronicles 22:19, 1 Chronicles 29:3).**

PRAYER

Dear Lord, Please be my strength, and please grant me an extra dose of energy to take care of all the priorities in my life, including my children. May my children put you first everyday of their lives. I pray that I will be diligent to follow through with caring for my responsibilities as well as my children, AMEN.

PUSHING THE LIMITS

SCRIPTURE 20

SCRIPTURE: (2 Corinthians 10:13 NKJV)

We, however, will not boast beyond measure, but within the limits of the sphere which God appointed us—a sphere which especially includes you.

DEEPER REFLECTION

But we will not boast of things without our measure, but we will not rejoice above measure. There is great darkness in the language here, arising from its brevity. But the general idea seems to be clear. Paul says that he had no audacity as they had to boast of things entirely beyond their own domain and their actual achievements and influence: and, especially, that he was not willing to enter other people's labors; or to boast of things that had been done by the mere influence of his name, and beyond the proper limits of his personal efforts. He did not boast that he had done anything where he had not been himself on the ground and worked assiduously to secure the object. They, not improbably, had boasted of what had been done at Corinth as if it were really their work, even though it had been done by the apostle himself.

A measure to reach even you - The sense is that "the limits assigned to me include you and therefore I can justly boast of what I have done among you as within my own field of work". Paul was the apostle to the Gentiles **(Acts 26:17)**; and therefore, he considered the whole country of Greece to be within limits assigned to him. Nobody, therefore, could blame him for going there as if he were an intruder; no one claims that he had gone beyond proper limits.

PRAYER

May we know your power and grace to overcome the obstacles in our lives. May the things that stand in our way become examples of your limitless power. Clothe us with power as we live our lives in your righteous name, AMEN.

REPUTATION

SCRIPTURE 21

SCRIPTURE: (Ecclesiastes 7:1 NKJV)

A good name is better than precious ointment, And the day of death than the day of one's birth.

DEEPER REFLECTION

The resemblance between reputation and smell provides a common metaphor: the contrast is between reputations, as an honorable achievement only wise people earn, and fragrant smell, as a sense gratification enjoyed by all people.

The connection of this verse with the previous verses is as follows: the man, who wants to know what is profitable for man and good in this life, is told to act in such a way as to normally secure a good reputation (i.e., act like a wise man), and teach yourself this hard lesson: consider the day of death as preferable to the day of birth. Although Solomon seems to feel strongly in some places **(Ecclesiastes 2:16; Ecclesiastes 3:19-2)** that natural fear of death which is, to a great extent, the distrust founded on ignorance that Christ dispelled; However, he affirms the advantage of death over life with respect to his freedom from work, oppression, restlessness, and regarding its implication of an immediate and closer approach to God. While Solomon preferred the day of death, he could still have regarded birth as a good thing and had its place in God's creation.

PRAYER

Lord Please protect my name and my children reputation. Lord, restore and renew our strength, positivity. also enable them to be positive influencers for Your glory. Let them spread Your love to their community. May their friends catch a glimpse of who You are through their actions. Let them be salt and light to the world around them, AMEN.

SELF IMAGE

SCRIPTURE 22

SCRIPTURE: (Romans 12:2 NKJV)

And do not be conformed to this world, but be transformed by the renewing of your mind, that you may prove what is that good and acceptable and perfect will of God.

DEEPER REFLECTION

Transform yourselves....appear as a new person, and with new habits, since God has given you a new form of worship, so that you serve in the newness of the spirit, and not in the antiquity of the letter. The word implies a radical, complete, and universal change, both external and internal. This shows us the force of this word when used in a moral sense. It says, "I perceive myself not only modified, but transformed" that is, completely renewed. **(Romans 13:14)**

For the renewal of your mind... May the inner change produce the outer. Where the spirit, the temper, and the disposition of the mind, **(Ephesians 4:23),** are not renewed, an outward change is of little value and of short duration.

And perfect... finished and complete: when the mind is

renewed, and all life changes, then the will of God is perfectly fulfilled; because this is his great design in reference to every human being.

PRAYER

Dear God, Speak loudly to me and reveal all limiting images in my mind. Replace them with pictures that glorify you and accurately represent my full potential. Upgrade my opinion of myself and my vision for the future. Help my children realized that you made them so wonderfully complex! It is amazing to think about. Your workmanship is marvelous—and how well we know it. Thank You for choosing us before the foundation of the world, AMEN.

SPEECH

SCRIPTURE 23

SCRIPTURE: (Colossians 4:6 NKJV)

Let your speech always be with grace, seasoned with salt, that you may know how you ought to answer each one.

DEEPER REFLECTION

Let your speech always be with grace, "in Grace, or with respect to grace": let grace be the theme of your speech and conversation. When the saints meet together, they should converse with one another about the work of grace upon their souls, how it began, and how it has been carried on, and in what case it is now; They should speak of the great things and wonders of grace, which God has done for them, what would be comfortable and edifying for them, and do to the glory of God's grace. Therefore, all obscene words, expressions of conditioning, nonsense talking and jesting should not be used. Or this may consider the manner of speech, and the language of the saints; It should be in the exercise of grace; It should be in truth, fidelity and sincerity, without lying, dissimulation, and flattery; It should be consistent with the grace of love, so that evil must not have been spoken one of the others for this is contrary to love, and so not to grace: and what is said, must have been spoken in fear of God; The reason so many evil things come out of the mouths of men is that the fear of God is not in them.

PRAYER

Heavenly Lord, may the words of our mouth and the actions of our heart reflect only the grace you have demonstrated to all mankind. Lord, give my children pure thoughts so that their speech may influence others ,and therefore set them apart for your kingdom. In Jesus Name, AMEN.

STEWARDSHIP

SCRIPTURE 24

SCRIPTURE: (Proverbs 27:18 NKJV)

Whoever keeps the fig tree will eat its fruit; so he who waits on his master will be honored.

DEEPER REFLECTION

The relationship that subsists between us and our Lord - He is our Master. You are men, and naturally you are moved by everything that moves other men, but still, the main driving force for you who are Christians is the supremacy of Christ. He has a right to be our Master from the very dignity of His character. We render service to Him because of His love for us. And our position as servants is irreversible. If even the one who keeps a fig tree is rewarded with a part of its fruits, surely the one who has the most honorable office of serving his master will be honored by that master. **(Psalm 123:2, 1 Samuel 2:30).**

PRAYER

Gracious and loving God, we understand that you call us to be the stewards of your abundance, the caretakers of all you have entrusted to us. Help us always to use your gifts wisely. May our faithful stewardship bear witness to the love of Christ in our lives, AMEN.

STRESS

SCRIPTURE 25

SCRIPTURE: (Psalms 28:7 NKJV)

The LORD is my strength and my shield; My heart trusted in Him, and I am helped; Therefore my heart greatly rejoices, And with my song I will praise Him.

DEEPER REFLECTION

The Lord is my strength, that is, the author of both natural and spiritual force; that gave us the strength of body and fortitude of mind to withstand all the exercises in which we attempted ourselves; The force of our life, spiritual and temporal, and of our salvation; the strength of our heart under present anguish, and that we knew it would be so in the hour of death, when our heart and our strength would fail.

And they help me: This was the fruit of their trust, even a gracious experience of divine assistance: the saints are helpless in themselves, and they are also helpless. Of man; God is their only helper; He helps them out of all their problems; in what he calls them, and what they want; and the help he gives is sometimes quick, and always capable; And sometimes by means, and sometimes without them.

PRAYER

Loving God, please grant me peace of mind and calm my troubled heart. My soul is like a turbulent sea. Give me the strength and clarity of mind to find my purpose and walk the path you've laid out for me. God, today my children and I will choose to trust you, because we know that you are with us. Please strengthen us and help us, empower them to cast down any thought that would want to cause them stress, anxiety, or fear, AMEN.

TECHNOLOGY

SCRIPTURE 26

SCRIPTURE: (Jeremiah 10:12 NKJV)

He has made the earth by His power, He has established the world by His wisdom, and has stretched out the heavens at His discretion.

DEEPER REFLECTION

Technology is a mixed bag of blessings and curses. On the other hand, it has solved numerous problems around the world, it has alleviated many diseases, and it has improved the quality of life for billions of people. On the other hand, technology can be used to inflict pain and suffering, and it can lead to unintended consequences.

Technology must be redeemed for the glory of God, your good, and the good of others. Technology cannot be simply rejected, demonized, or even mindlessly accepted and used. It is a vehicle to share the gospel and do good for others.

PRAYER

Lord, we pray that technology may be the servant, not the controller of our lives. Help me to set my affections on things above rather than on things of the world. Help us use technology to mature in our relationship with You and to develop into the happy, joyful, strong Christian that we have the potential to be. In Jesus Name, AMEN.

TIME MANAGEMENT

SCRIPTURE 27

SCRIPTURE: (Ephesians 5:15-17 NKJV)

See then that you walk circumspectly, not as fools but as wise, redeeming the time, because the days are evil. Therefore do not be unwise, but understand what the will of the Lord is.

DEEPER REFLECTION

See then that you are fit to rebuke sin in others; than yourselves, on whom the light of Christ already shines; walk with circumspection with precision, with the greatest accuracy; doing His will, as it was made known to you in His word, your rule, and His glory your end, in all your actions, concerns, labors, and pursuits; paying the utmost attention to every step, and behaving, not like fools, who do not understand their duty or interest, and who do not consider what they are doing, how they are advancing, or where it will end; but as wise men who know the value of their immortal souls, the snares that their subtle and powerful enemies have laid or will lay to ensnare them, the many pressing dangers they must avoid, and the important ends they must achieve.

Therefore, since the times are so bad and the danger so great; Be not foolish, ignorant of your duty and true interest, neglectful of the concerns of your immortal souls, and inconsiderate as before; but understanding what the will of the Lord is at all times, places and circumstances.

PRAYER

As I walk through my day, I ask that you would reveal these snares that are set up to keep me from walking in your best for me. Thank you for showing me your path and for your patience with me. I pray that my children manage school, activities, family, and time with the Lord in a way that best honors God and brings his perfect wisdom.In Jesus' name, AMEN.

UNITY

SCRIPTURE 28

SCRIPTURE: (Psalm 133:1 NKJV)

A Song of Ascents. Of David. Behold, how good and how pleasant it is for brethren to dwell together in unity!

DEEPER REFLECTION

The excellence of brotherly love. - We can't say too much, outside well enough if it can be said, to persuade people to live together in peace. It is good for us, for our honor and comfort; and brings constant delight to those who live in unity. The kindness of this is likened to holy anointing oil. This is the fruit of the Spirit, the proof of our union with Christ, and it adorns His gospel. It's profitable as well as enjoyable; it brings numerous blessings like drops of dew. **(Genesis 13:8).**

Believers who live in love and peace will have the God of love and peace with them now, and will shortly be with him forever, in the world of infinite love and peace. May all who love the Lord forbear and forgive one another, as God, for the love of Christ, has forgiven them.**(Hebrews 13:1).**

PRAYER

Compassionate and gracious God, all tribes and tongues will one day acknowledge Jesus as lord. Change our behavior and make us united. Help us to acknowledge every person as your creation. Today, we claim unity among our children, unite the hearts of your servants, and reveal to them Your great purpose. May they follow Your commandments and abide in Your law, AMEN.

DEALING WITH DOUBT

SCRIPTURE 29

SCRIPTURE: (James 1:6 NKJV)

But let him ask in faith, with no doubting, for he who doubts is like a wave of the sea driven and tossed by the wind.

DEEPER REFLECTION

But let him ask in faith. This shows here, first, the correct way to pray; because as we cannot pray without the word, as it were, leading the way, we must believe before we pray; because we testify with prayer that we hope to obtain from God the grace that he has promised. Thus, everyone who does not have faith in the promises prays secretly. Therefore, too, we learn what true faith is; James, having asked us to ask in faith, adds this explanation, not hesitating or wavering. So faith is what builds on God's promises and makes sure we get what we ask for. Therefore, it follows that it is connected with confidence and certainty regarding God's love towards us. **(Matthew 21:22)**

The one who shakes, or doubts. This expresses how God punishes the unbelief of those who doubt his promises; because, by their own restlessness, they are internally tormented; because there is never calm for their souls, except that they remember the truth of God. He finally concludes that such are not worthy to receive anything from God. **(1 Timothy 2:8)**

PRAYER

Lord, we long for the days when we will have perfect faith and trust and when we will not fear or doubt. Have mercy on us Lord, and increase our faith. When we doubt your will in our lives. Lord, help me to instill a spirit of strength and courage in my children, so they may trust in Your Word. Allow me to remind them to face life's problems with their eyes fixed in you rather than trying to fix everything themselves. Oh Lord, have mercy on us, AMEN.

FRIENDSHIP

SCRIPTURE 30

SCRIPTURE: (Proverbs 17:17 NKJV)

A friend loves at all times, and a brother is born for adversity.

DEEPER REFLECTION

In the biblical quote we find two key foundations to start establishing a true friendship based on love, and not on the disproportionate interests of genuine appreciation.

In every period, space, and place, beyond measuring time; the depth of this phrase is broken down into; love over any circumstance, difficulty, or lack. Genuine friendship is one that is shown in the worst moments, it is when it is most needed to be present. It is generally said to be a friend, in the good and beautiful moments of life, however, the demonstration of this bond is made in those moments when the disease appeared, where finances failed, where perhaps you have lost a loved one. In these times, the true meaning of what friendship is has been lost.

As I mentioned before, "friend" is derived from love, so you cannot say you are a friend if you do not love. God's design from the beginning of his creation was to establish friendship, based on its derivative. What is the derivative? Love, based on its perfect essence, that is love.

PRAYER

Lord please give my children love and blessings without end so that their hearts may reflect the goodness you placed in them. Lord, we pray that we may win souls through our friendship with others. Heavenly Father help my children to first love you with all their hearts and then to love their friends in the same way you love us. May the joy of the Lord radiates through them while they share your loving kindness, AMEN.

ADVERSITY

SCRIPTURE 31

SCRIPTURE: (Psalms 34:19 NKJV)

Many are the afflictions of the righteous, but the LORD delivers him out of them all.

DEEPER REFLECTION

Let the righteous seek more trouble than others, and likewise expect greater comfort than others; because when they are well, they will be eclipsed again, to show that their light was borrowed; and when they are eclipsed, their light will return, to show their difference from those whom God hates, who fall from plague to plague, as they run from sin to sin.

So, if you notice, when you go through an offense, and take a little wrong and suffer trouble in silence, you have a kind of peace and joy in your heart, as if you have won a victory, and the greater your patience, still, lesser is your pain. Because as a light load, carried at the end of the arm, it weighs much more than a load of three weights, if carried on the shoulders, which they are made to carry; so if a man grows impatient to carry his cross, which is not fit to bear, he will groan and murmur, and let the load fall on his head, like a broken staff, promising to help him over the water, and walk away with him in the ditch.(**Psalm 71:20, Psalm 71:20)**.

PRAYER

Dear Lord, help me to rest and stand in the Lord's peace, to relax and trust God and let him fight the invisible spiritual enemy with his peace. Please give my children stamina to handle trials and struggles that come and the faith to endure any hardship. Help them to hear Your voice, and feel Your presence, AMEN.

SECURITY

SCRIPTURE 32

SCRIPTURE: (Psalm 122:7 NKJV)

Peace be within your walls, Prosperity within your palaces.

DEEPER REFLECTION

God himself is a wall of fire around us; The salvation of Christ is like walls and ramparts to us; The power and providence of God protect us: Within these walls, God's people have a place and a name; All the inhabitants of Zion in common are included in this petition, and peace is wished to all; In the church militia, all the saints are soldiers and in a state of war; And here the success of his arms against sin, Satan and the world, is desired.**(Isaiah 62:6).**

As there were palaces in Jerusalem for the king, the nobles, and the great men in the land; so there is in the Church of God, where He is known, for a refuge; even the worst places in it are preferable to the palaces of the greatest capitals.**(Psalm 48:3)**.

PRAYER

Lord Jesus, Protect my family and me from trouble wherever we go, and keep evil far from us. Let your love and faithfulness, along with your goodness and mercy, surround us daily, so we will not fear whatever might come against us, AMEN.

IDENTITY

SCRIPTURE 33

SCRIPTURE: (Galatians 3:26 NKJV)

For you are all sons of God through faith in Christ Jesus.

DEEPER REFLECTION

True Christians enjoy great privileges under the gospel, and they are no longer considered servants, but sons; they are not now kept at such a distance, and under such restrictions, as the Jews were. Having accepted Christ Jesus as their Lord and Savior, and trusting in Him alone for their justification and salvation, they become children of God. But no external form or profession can secure these blessings; because if someone does not have the Spirit of Christ, it is not His. **(John 1:12).**

But by faith in Christ Jesus; It is not that faith makes children of God, or puts them in such a relationship; No, that is God's own act and deed; of his free grace and kindness. God the Father predestined His elect to the adoption of children, and has secured and established this blessing for them in the Covenant of Grace **(Romans 8:16)** since a spirit of adoption has a strong reason and argument, showing that they are not under the law like a school teacher, in which the apostle here establishes the light; since they are children and not servants, and so free from the bondage of the law.

PRAYER

Lord, help me see the minute I start placing my identity in something else- my children, my career, my marriage, my gifts and talents. Help me keep you before me in all things. Teach my children that they have the opportunity to accept a new, beautiful identity that is called good. Let them not place their self-worth in accomplishments achieved, but let our children discover these deeper truths about who You believe they are and build every decision they make on that sure foundation. In Jesus' Name, AMEN.

GOALS

SCRIPTURE 34

SCRIPTURE: (Philippians 4:13 NKJV)

I can do all things through Christ who strengthens me.

DEEPER REFLECTION

I can do all things through Christ. As he had boasted of things that were very good, so that this cannot be attributed to pride or provide others with an occasion for foolish boasting, he adds, that it is by Christ who is endowed with this strength. "I can do all things," he says, "but it is in Christ, not by my own power, because it is Christ who gives me strength." Therefore, we infer that Christ will be no less strong and invincible in us too, if we are aware of our own weakness, and we trust only in His power. When he says all things, he means simply those things that pertain to his calling. Through Christ we can achieve all our goals **(Ephesians 3:16, John 15:4-7).**

PRAYER

Lord Jesus, I submit each and every goal to you. May my goals reflect your will for my life, and may they glorify you. I pray for other people who have goals and dreams that they desire to achieve. May my children goals always align fully to your plan for their lives. I pray that they will be obedient to the leading to the Holy Spirit. That things would end well for them, that the purpose and goals of their lives will be fulfilled. That every detail, every hurt, betrayal, would work out for divine purpose in Jesus name, I pray, AMEN.

DETERMINATION

SCRIPTURE 35

SCRIPTURE: (Isaiah 8:10 NKJV)

Take counsel together, but it will come to nothing; Speak the word, but it will not stand, for God is with us.

DEEPER REFLECTION

Having spoken of the forces of the enemies, he now comes to his advice; as he had said: "Although enemies may abound not only in armor and strength, but in counsel and wisdom, they will still accomplish nothing." And this warning was much needed; because it often happens that we despise enemies, however powerful and well-armed, because they want advice and are guided by blind violence and not by reason. **(Romans 8:31)**

I have decreed it decree a decree. This relates to your impudence, or is the conclusion of the query; because after deliberation, a decree generally follows. He declares that all these things will go up in smoke. But by determining within ourselves and God also promising he will be with us, we can overcome any trials and temptations without looking back. **(1 Corinthians 16:13)**

PRAYER

Oh Lord, help me to be on guard so that I can stand firm in my faith. I know that standing firm requires me to be determined and motivated, so Lord I pray for your help in this area of my life. Through conscious awareness of God in all, I envision that my children will have a strong determination and will for your kingdom, free of discomfort, hopelessness, anxiety, negative self-talk, and seeming limitations, AMEN.

SUBMISSION

SCRIPTURE 36

SCRIPTURE: (James 4:7 NKJV)

Therefore submit to God. Resist the devil and he will flee from you.

DEEPER REFLECTION

Send your understanding of God's truth; to submit your wills to the will of His command, the will of His providence. Submit to God, because He is willing to do good. (Ephesians 6:11).

However, the promise that he adds, respecting Satan's flight, seems to be refuted by daily experience; for it is true that the more strenuously he resists, the more he is urged. For Satan, in a way, he acts playfully when he is not seriously repelled; but against those who really resist him, he uses all the strength he possesses. And besides, he is never tired of fighting; but when he is conquered in one battle, he immediately engages in another. To this, I reply that fleeing must be taken here to put to flight or route. And, without a doubt, although he repeats his attacks continuously, he always walks away defeated. **(Ephesians 4:27, Matthew 4:3-11)**.

PRAYER

Most Holy and gracious Lord, we submit our will to you. We give up our agenda and our plan for yours. I submit myself to You! I pray that my children will come to a knowledge of the truth of the Lord Jesus Christ, crucified and risen from the dead for their forgiveness and will submit themselves to you. Help us trust in your plans, AMEN.

DIGNITY

SCRIPTURE 37

SCRIPTURE: (Proverbs 31:25 NKJV)

Strength and honor are her clothing; She shall rejoice in time to come.

DEEPER REFLECTION

Strength, not of the body, but of the mind. The church is clothed with strength, as her Lord, head, and husband, is said to be, **(Psalm 93:10)**; and that she has of him; because she is the weakest ship, and weak in herself, but she is strong in him; and she is able to endure and do all things, with a strength of mind to endure all enemies, and perseveres in the pit, and she is clothed with "honor"; In honorable garments, suitable for her rank and dignity; In cloth of gold, in sewing of dress; With the garments of salvation, and the robe of justice.

All your need is supplied by Christ; they hope for his death, and then rejoice and sing, "O death, where is your sting?"**(1 Corinthians 15:55)**; They will have confidence on the day of judgment, and they will not be ashamed; he will come to Zion with everlasting joy; and he will rejoice with Christ, the angels and the saints, to all eternity.

PRAYER

Loving God, Creator of dignity and all that lives, Help us to be bridges. Help us cry out for respect and value for all when society forgets that we are all God's children in our most basic nature. Help us to bear witness to the dignity of all whom you have created, regardless of stage of life, or wealth, or ability, or color, or creed, for every person, AMEN.

FEAR OF THE LORD

SCRIPTURE 38

SCRIPTURE: (Proverbs 8:13 NKJV)

The fear of the LORD is to hate evil; Pride and arrogance and the evil way and the perverse mouth I hate.

DEEPER REFLECTION

The fear of the Lord that he had previously said was the beginning of wisdom; it is to hate evil. It consists of careful abstinence from all sin, and not for carnal or prudential reasons, but because of a real hatred towards it, due to its contradiction with nature and divine attributes, its opposition to the word and will of God, its infinite evil in itself and its eternally destructive consequences; Pride which he mentions first, as what most God hates, and the most opposed to true wisdom, and to the genuine fear of God, which constantly produces humility; and the wicked way, all wicked actions, especially sinful ways and customs; and the wicked mouth, I hate false doctrines, bad advice and deceit. **(Psalm 97:10)**

Also, the fear of the Lord is to hate evil as it is impossible to hate evil without loving good; and how the hatred of evil will lead man to abandon the evil path; and the love of good will lead him to do what is right in the sight of God, under the influence of that Spirit which has given hatred to evil and inspired the love of good: this, therefore, implies the sum and substance of the true religion, here called the fear of the Lord. **(Proverbs 16:6, Psalm 97:10, Proverbs 16:6)**

PRAYER

Lord Jesus, today, I want to choose to walk in the fear of the Lord so that my family and I can be blessed all the days of our life. As I place my children in your mighty, loving hands, give me peace, knowing that you are right by their side. Lord, instill in them a reverent fear of You as our just and loving Heavenly Father. May their reverence for You keep them on the godly path in all their lives, AMEN.

SELFLESSNESS

SCRIPTURE 39

SCRIPTURE: (Romans 12:10 NKJV)

Be kindly affectionate to one another with brotherly love, in honor giving preference to one another.

DEEPER REFLECTION

Be kindly affectionate to one another with brotherly love; this is a branch of that love, before it is counseled, which should be without, if not serious, and without guile and deceit. The objects of this grace are "brothers", not in that sense, since all the descendants of Adam are, or men of the same country, or as such who are born of the same parents in a natural sense are; to each of whom love is due under their respective characters and relationships: But such that they meet in a spiritual sense, that they are born of God, they are of His family, they belong to His family, they are the brothers of Christ, and the more and they are members of the same church, incorporated together in the same state of the church, or at least members of Christ, and of the universal Church. Now the love of these should be kind, tender and loving, reciprocal and mutual; such should love one another;

There should be no love wanting on both sides; and it must be universal, and reach all the saints, though of different gifts, light, knowledge, and experience, or whether high or low, rich or poor; and he must show himself carrying burdens, with each other, and pushing each other, forgiving each other, and building each other up in their most sacred faith, and praying with each other. **(John 13:34, 1 Peter 2:17)**

PRAYER

Dear Lord, please help us to feel your Spirit deep within our hearts. Help us to feel your strength and to choose selflessness over selfishness. Help us to truly want to show compassion and kindness to other people, AMEN.

WORTH

SCRIPTURE 40

SCRIPTURE: (Matthew 10:31 NKJV)

Do not fear therefore; you are of more value than many sparrows.

DEEPER REFLECTION

When Christ is accepted as your Lord and Savior, in addition to passing from death to life, a man goes from being a creature to becoming a son of God, and as His son, he is also an heir to His kingdom.(**1 Peter 2:9).** It is not the achievements or their own merits that make a person valuable, the true value that someone may have lies in the great love that God has for him. **(Matthew 10:29-31).**

God has so much love for His children that He has decided to spend eternity with them. He has sent his son to prepare the abode for all those who love Him and seek Him from the heart. You are not just any person, and you have been predestined to a beautiful life next to your Heavenly Father! **(John 14:2-3).**

PRAYER

You call me yours, worthy, precious. Forgive me for accepting the false identities that attempt to draw me away from you. I pray You would guide honorable influences into my children's lives, giving them solid examples of right standing up for themselves and knowing their worth. Hear me O Lord! AMEN.

CALLING

SCRIPTURE 41

SCRIPTURE: (John 15:16 NKJV)

You did not choose me, but I chose you and appointed you that you would go and bear fruit, and that your fruit would remain, so that whatever you ask of the Father in My name He may give to you.

DEEPER REFLECTION

O ineffable grace! What were we before Christ chose us, if not miserable and abandoned creatures? That's how we were, but now we are chosen to be good by the grace of the one who chose us.

Furthermore, since we are completely useless servants, those who appear to be the most excellent of all will not be fit for the smallest calling until they have been chosen. However, the higher the degree of honor to which someone has been raised, remember that he has deeper obligations to God.

And I have named you. The election is hidden until it is made known, when a man receives an office to which he had been appointed; Like Paul, in the passage that he quoted a little while ago, he says that he had been separated from his mother's womb, he adds that he was created an apostle because he pleased God very much. His words are: ***When it pleased God, who separated me from my mother's womb, and called me by his grace,*** **(Galatians 1:15 KJV).**

PRAYER

God, I ask that you reveal our individual calling to us. Show us our future path, and make us recipients of Your warnings Lord, break our hearts for the things that break yours. Show us the needs of those around us, AMEN.

INTEGRITY

SCRIPTURE 42

SCRIPTURE: (Proverbs 20:7 NKJV)

The righteous man walks in his integrity; His children are blessed after him.

DEEPER REFLECTION

The just walks in his integrity, he who in his innocence behaves with righteousness, this is the faithful and upright man, who becomes just by the obedience of Christ; and walks by faith in him, and according to the truth of the Gospel. ***His children are blessed after him,*** if they follow him in his righteousness, with temporal blessings; and, walking in the same integrity as he does, they are blessed with spiritual blessings and eternal blessing. The blessing of the Lord falls on them for a thousand generations,(**Exodus 20: 6; Deuteronomy 7:9).**

Our integrity can be God's means of saving our sons and daughters. If they see the truth of our religion tested by our lives, they may believe in Jesus for themselves. Lord, I want the fulfillment of this word in my house!

PRAYER

Dear Lord Jesus, You were the one who said, "let the children come to me for of such is the kingdom of heaven." I thank you for my children and the way that they learn about you in their daily lives. I ask that in your grace, we may grow in wisdom and integrity and understand the importance of honesty and truth, AMEN.

REVENGE

SCRIPTURE 43

SCRIPTURE: (Romans 12:19 NKJV)

Beloved, do not avenge yourselves, but rather give place to wrath; for it is written, "Vengeance is Mine, I will repay," says the Lord.

DEEPER REFLECTION

Ever since men became enemies of God, they have been very willing to be enemies of one another. And those who embrace religion must expect to meet enemies in a world whose smiles seldom match those of Christ. Do not repay anyone evil for evil. That is a brutal reward, which only corresponds to animals, who are not aware of any being above them, nor of any existence in the future. And do not only do, but study and take care to do what is lovable and trustworthy, and recommend religion to all with whom you converse. Study the things that promote peace; if possible, without offending God or hurting the conscience. Do not avenge yourself. This is a hard lesson for corrupt nature, so a remedy against it is added. Give place to anger. When a man's passion rises, and the current is strong, let it pass; lest he is further infuriated against us. The line of our duty is clearly drawn, and if our enemies are not melted by persevering kindness, we must not seek revenge. **(Leviticus 19:18, Deuteronomy 32:35).**

PRAYER

Lord Jesus, fight those who fight against us! Take your shield and armor and come to our rescue. Lift up your spear and war against those who pursue my family and me. Promise that you will save us. May those who try to kill me be defeated and disgraced! AMEN.

CONFRONTATION

SCRIPTURE 44

SCRIPTURE: (Psalm 18:18 NKJV)

They confronted me in the day of my disaster, but the LORD was my support.

DEEPER REFLECTION

When was the last time someone confronted you with your sin? How did you handle it? When was the last time you had to confront someone with their sin? Did you try to avoid it? The very thought of confronting or reprimanding someone can be a very uncomfortable one. However, the concept is an essential part of God's plan for the Christian community and for spiritual growth. **(Hebrews 3:13)**

So why is biblical confrontation so difficult for us? First, we have misconstrued confrontation as negative when it should be positive. The word "exhort" means to encourage. Our message in confrontation should encourage others to do good deeds, not discourage them: "don't give up! There is hope and help for you! The good life is found within the limits of God's Word! Believe in the promises of the Bible!"

So the next time you're confronted, fire your identity attorney and be honest about your sin. And when God calls you to confront someone, be gentle and an ambassador.

PRAYER

Lord, give me a heart of mercy. Help me stay positive amid of negativity. I pray against conflict and unnecessary confrontation in every family relationship. Let my family be founded upon Your awesome love Lord, AMEN.

PRIDE

SCRIPTURE 45

SCRIPTURE: (James 4:6 NKJV)

But He gives more grace. Therefore He says: God resists the proud, But gives grace to the humble.

DEEPER REFLECTION

Pride is the lack of truth about our position and importance in the world. Proud people would like to be the most important. Of course, you can't. But you can fool yourself about your ranking position. You may convince yourself that your impact on the march of life is greater than it actually is. That makes you feel powerful. He can't bear to think that someone could have more influence than him on events. He wants to totally control his life, without asking anyone for anything. Although it is difficult, the proud may not be proud and may even be grateful. He can recognize the merit of his parents or his educators in having made him as it is and thank them, but he thinks that once he has become what he is, his imprint on the world will be greater than that of anyone who has helped him get to where he is. At his highest degree, he vomits up the very idea of God.

Humility and prayer are the antidotes to the three sins of vanity, pride and arrogance. *"**Humility is living in truth**.* And so it is. He who lives in truth knows his true worth. **(Proverbs 29:23)**

PRAYER

Father, you hate pride, so deliver me from it. Never let me be convinced that my fortresses are my strengths. You're my strength and my security. May my children be humble, and keep them from the disgrace that comes from pride, AMEN.

REBELLION

SCRIPTURE 46

SCRIPTURE: (Proverbs 17:11 NKJV)

An evil man seeks only rebellion; therefore a cruel messenger will be sent against him.

DEEPER REFLECTION

Rebellion is disobedience to God and is compared to the spirit of divination. This is an important parallel because divination is what pagan cultures practice in hopes of communicating with spirits for answers. God warns us that these practices are prohibited since He is our source. Thus, the rebellion is established in the pride that says: "I don't need you, God. I will find answers to my questions without your help and approval. Then I'll start influencing people with what I know and get all the glory."

Rebellion wants to be worshiped and obeyed instead of relationship and submission to God. Rebellion cuts off your Kingdom privileges, but by God's grace, a rebellious person can still have access to God through Jesus Christ. The purpose of the spirit of rebellion is to keep a believer from prospering. **(2 Samuel 16:5-9).**

PRAYER

Father, right now, I repent of any rebellion in my own life, and I ask You to forgive me and show me any areas where rebellion exists, so that I can root it out of my life forever with Your supernatural help. I know that the spirit of rebellion is a demonic spirit and has no right and no place in my children. So, by the authority You have given me, through Christ Jesus, I command every wrong spirit, including the spirit of rebellion, to leave my children right now in the Name of Jesus, AMEN.

SERVICING OTHERS

SCRIPTURE 47

SCRIPTURE: (Proverbs 25:21 NKJV)

If your enemy is hungry, give him bread to eat; and if he is thirsty, give him water to drink.

DEEPER REFLECTION

It is well known by all that the perfect commandment is summed up in love for God, ourselves, and others, in the same way that God loved us. Well, now God reveals one of the most identifying aspects of the love that He demands of us. This aspect is: The service.

The issue here is to understand how to do it. How do we serve God and others? What is the motivation to do it? What is the correct way to do it? The fundamental thing is to know that the service to God must be born from our hearts. In other words, service is an attitude of the heart.

There are great examples of love and service that show that both must always go hand in hand. They are a very effective antidote against anything that wants to contaminate the heart. **(Exodus 23:4-5, Proverbs 24:17).**

PRAYER

Heavenly Father, thank you for giving us such a great example of what it means to serve each other. Help us use the gifts that you have given us to serve others everyday. Pray that they would serve others around them with all their heart and that they would learn to put the needs of others before their own. God, please help my children serve wholeheartedly, as if they were serving the Lord, not men, AMEN.

TEMPERANCE

SCRIPTURE 48

SCRIPTURE: (Galatians 5:23 NKJV)

Gentleness, self-control. Against such there is no law.

DEEPER REFLECTION

It is being under the control of the Holy Spirit. Temperance or self-control is the inner force that controls our passions and desires. We must walk in the Spirit. If we walk in the flesh, according to our desires or thoughts, what will arise in the face of temptation or difficulty, or aggression will be our fallen nature, our self. It generally offers little resistance.

Temperance or self-control gives us control over decisions. We must exercise self-control with the help of the Holy Spirit. Some worry about eating healthy to stay healthy, and that's fine, since we are the temple of the Holy Spirit. **(Proverbs 16:23-24 and James 3:5-6).**

The Word of God says that the tongue is small but boasts of great things and that it contaminates the whole body. Doctors have proven that a person, by what he speaks or thinks, can influence his body because he sends orders to his central nervous system. "I am tired: I have no strength, I cannot do anything", and the nerve center says: "yes, it is true". We must go back to God's Word and use his language that is creative, uplifting, and victorious.

PRAYER

Let temperance grow in me and lead me to discover other virtues that bring deeper union with you. Temper my desires, O Lord, and turn my focus towards you. Help my children to learn to control their thoughts, feelings, and actions and to desire what is good and reject what is evil. In your sacred name, I pray, AMEN.

ACCOUNTABILITY

SCRIPTURE 49

SCRIPTURE: (Romans 14:12 NKJV)

So then each of us shall give account of himself to God.

DEEPER REFLECTION

Christians should not judge or despise others, because both one and the other have little to account for. To believe as regards the judgment of the great day, would be mute rash judging. Let each search in his own heart and life; he who is strict in judging and humiliating himself will not be fit to judge and despise his brother. We must be careful not to say or do things that may cause others to stumble or fall. The one means one, the other greater to a lesser degree of the offense; what can be a reason for sorrow or blame our brother?

We will not be obliged, before the tribunal of God, to give an account of the conduct of each one; each one will account for himself; and try to be prepared to give an account with joy. **(Ecclesiastes 11:9, Matthew 12:36, Matthew 18:23)**.

PRAYER

Teach us your ways and guide us with Your Holy Spirit. Lord, we want to be accountable to you. Give us a teachable Spirit and a desire to apply all the truths that we are discovering. You hold me accountable to grow in grace and in a knowledge of the Lord Jesus, by faith in Christ and not by trusting in my own abilities, and for that I thank you. In Jesus' name we pray, AMEN.

OVERCOMING SIN

SCRIPTURE 50

SCRIPTURE: (Revelation 3:21 NKJV)

To him who overcomes I will grant to sit with me on My throne, as I also overcame and sat down with My Father on His throne.

DEEPER REFLECTION

The first resource the Bible mentions to help us overcome sin is the Holy Spirit. The Holy Spirit is a gift that God has given us to be victorious in Christian living. In **Galatians 5:16-25**, God makes a contrast between the works of the flesh and the fruit of the Spirit. In that passage, we are called to walk in the Spirit.

We can also overcome sin through God's word. **2 Timothy 3:16-17** says that God has given us His Word to equip us for every good deed. This teaches us how to live and what to believe, reveals to us when we have chosen the wrong paths, helps us get back on the right path, and helps us stay on that path.

A third essential resource in our battle against sin is prayer. Again, this is a resource that Christians mention lip service but do not put into practice; they make very poor use of it. We have prayer meetings, prayer times, etc., but we don't use prayer in the same way the early church did. God has given us wonderful promises concerning prayer **(Matthew 7:7-11; Luke 18:1-8; John 6:23-27; 1 John 5:14-15).**

Many Christians find that having an accountability partner can greatly benefit in overcoming difficult sins. Having another person with whom you can talk, pray, be encouraged, and even be reprimanded is of great value. Temptation is common to all of us **(1 Corinthians 10:13)**. Having a partner or a group with whom we are accountable can give us the final dose of encouragement and motivation we need to overcome even the strongest of sins.

PRAYER

Lord, everyday you give me a new beginning. Help me to ride each new wave of temptation, and to overcome the sins that can drag my life down. Father, in the name of Jesus Christ, I come to you desiring my children to be free from all generational sins, iniquities, and their results, which may have an influence upon my children. I thank you for saving us and cleansing us of my sin. I confess that we belong to you, AMEN.

OVERCOMING TEMPTATION

SCRIPTURE 51

SCRIPTURE: (Matthew 26:41 NKJV)

Watch and pray, lest you enter into temptation. The spirit indeed is willing, but the flesh is weak.

DEEPER REFLECTION

We go through life with the mentality that temptations are only for evil; their only purpose is to be an obstacle in our spiritual life. But, what we don't realize is that temptation is present in our daily lives to teach us to do good, a springboard to lead us into a deeper relationship with Christ. Today, we must look at temptation with a different perception.

Temptation with a choice. That choice will be to resist temptation or to follow the characteristics of Christ: to bear the fruit of the Spirit by the operation of the Holy Spirit in our lives **(Galatians 5:22–23).** Just as fruit takes a while to branch and grow, temptation tries to bear spiritual fruit in our lives, but after a process of time.

Satan uses temptation to discourage and defeat the child of God. He knows where to tempt us, how often, and with what.

But, we must always be vigilant and be aware of his schemes, lest he surprises us **(II Corinthians 2:11).** We can use temptations for our good!

PRAYER

Heavenly and merciful Father, I can no longer make it alone in this world. Lord, I need you each and every second, every minute, every hour of my life. Guide my actions, my thoughts, my words, my deeds. Allow me not to yield to temptation. Please, Lord, give my children the wisdom to walk away when they are tempted, and the clarity to see the way out that you will provide, AMEN.

OVERCOMING BAD ATTITUDES

SCRIPTURE 52

SCRIPTURE: (Ephesians 4:31 NKJV)

Let all bitterness, wrath, anger, clamor, and evil speaking be put away from you, with all malice.

DEEPER REFLECTION

That is all the bitterness. Again we condemn anger; but, on the present occasion, we see in relation to him those crimes by which he is usually accompanied, such as noisy disputes and reproaches. Between anger and wrath, there is little difference, except that the former denotes power and the latter deed; but here, the only difference is that anger is a more sudden attack. Correcting everything else will go a long way in removing the malice. With this term, it expresses that mental depravity that is opposed to humanity and justice, and that is generally called malignancy. **(Psalm 37:8, Colossians 3:8).**

PRAYER

Lord, free me from the shackles of a bad attitude. Work in my heart and mind to transform my thinking from negative to positive. When things are getting out of control with my life and my children, Lord I need You to step in and bring your peace. Please bring forth your ease and stability to any situation we may face, AMEN.

OVERCOMING BODY IMAGE ISSUES

SCRIPTURE 53

SCRIPTURE: (Psalm 139:14 NKJV)

I will praise you, for I am fearfully and wonderfully made; Marvelous are your works, and that my soul knows very well.

DEEPER REFLECTION

I am fearfully and wonderfully made- the texture of the human body is the most complicated and curious thing that can be conceived. It is, indeed, wonderfully done; and moreover, it is so exquisitely pleasing and delicate, that the slightest accident may in a moment damage or destroy some of those parts essentially necessary to the continuance of life; therefore, we are terribly made.

And God has done it to show us our fragility, so that we walk with death, keeping life in view; and feel the need to depend on the omniscient and continuous care and providence of God. **(Psalm 104:24, Psalm 92:4-5)**

PRAYER

Father, I pray today that you renew my mind and renew my thoughts concerning my body, my looks, my worth, and my value. I pray for my children's self-image. Help them to know that they are created in your image. You created and formed them, and they are wonderfully made by you. When they look at themselves, I pray that they will see who you created them to be. Call them by name, and remind them each day that they belong to you, AMEN.

OVERCOMING REJECTION

SCRIPTURE 54

SCRIPTURE: (John 15:18 NKJV)

If the world hates you, you know that it hated me before it hated you.

DEEPER REFLECTION

The world knows not God, and hence rejects the Church, which is in possession of this knowledge. Had the world known God, it would have recognized among Christians the tokens of the Divine presence and operation. Christians are not of the world. The world loves its own, but rejects that which is out of harmony with it. If Christians do not adopt the world's spirit and language and habits, this singularity and nonconformity naturally excite dislike and provoke ill-treatment.

It cannot but be that the world must be rebuked by the presence of the Church, confronting and reproving it. Whether by a public protest against the world's sins, or by the silent protest of a pure and upright life, Christians are bound to a course of action which will bring down upon them, now and again, the enmity and the anger of the world. **(Proverbs 29:27, Matthew 10:22)**

PRAYER

I am set free from the spirit of rejection, I am an overcomer and have victory through our Lord Jesus Christ. I know you wait with wide open arms, and see each child as precious. Today, I pray that through You my children will know their true worth and value in face of rejection, AMEN.

OVERCOMING GRUDGES

SCRIPTURE 55

SCRIPTURE: (Leviticus 19:18 NKJV)

You shall not take vengeance, nor bear any grudge against the children of your people, but you shall love your neighbor as yourself: I am the LORD.

DEEPER REFLECTION

Elsewhere we read: "Vengeance is mine, and I will pay." Therefore, do not snatch the sword of God out of His hand, do not sit on His seat, and do not make yourself a god for fear of the end. Well, let it go then, I'm not going to take revenge, but I'll surely remember it; I can forgive, but never forget, etc. See what follows in the next words of this verse: "Neither will you remember the wrong against the sons of your people.

So, you see, "remember" is condemned just like "avenge", and therefore, you must forgive and forget, or else the Lord will forget you from His Book of Life. No, look further: all this is still not enough, but we must "love our neighbor also, and that as ourselves", or else we will perish. Because, "I am the Lord", says the verse, that is, one who sees and hates and will strike you with that force that you cannot resist or bear. Foolish politics, think, then, of piety, and abhor that policy that devours piety and destroys you. You cannot live forever, but you must die and come to judgment. **(Deuteronomy 32:25, Exodus 23:4-5).**

PRAYER

Prince of Peace, thank you that you hear and answer our prayers. Today we come before you as we are experiencing anger and resentment and ask you to bless us with perfect peace. With Your help Lord, guide my children so they may overcome grudges, paralyze their resentment, and bitterness. Help them to let go and release these toxic emotions with the help of the Holy Spirit, AMEN.

OVERCOMING CONFLICT

SCRIPTURE 56

SCRIPTURE: (Proverbs 15:1 NKJV)

A soft answer turns away wrath, but a harsh word stirs up anger.

DEEPER REFLECTION

The tongue of the wise uses knowledge correctly. This means that, opportunely, it is the right time and place, or illustrates it, makes it beautiful and pleasant, such as Proverbs 15:13. The wise man not only has knowledge, but can give it proper expression **(Proverbs 16:23).** "The tongue of the wise adorns wisdom." The tongue of the wise uses knowledge correctly. This means that, opportunely, the wise man praises wisdom and makes it acceptable to his hearers by producing his feelings and opinions in proper language and on proper occasions. "The tongue of the wise knows what is just, But the mouth of fools utters folly **(Proverbs 15:28).** A fool cannot open his mouth without exposing his madness; he speaks without due consideration or discretion; as the Vulgate calls it, ebullient, "bubbles", like a boiling pot, which emits its contents untimely and uselessly. "The mouth of fools proclaims evil."

We can overcome conflict by giving smooth words and answer to our partners, family, children, and co-workers **(Proverbs 28:25).**

PRAYER

We have lost track as a family because of pain and pride. We have hurt each other through our actions and words. Lord, let your love take control of our thoughts, actions, and words as we interact with each other toady and forever more, AMEN.

OVERCOMING ENVY

SCRIPTURE 57

SCRIPTURE: (Proverbs 6:34 NKJV)

For jealousy is a husband's fury; therefore he will not spare in the day of vengeance.

DEEPER REFLECTION

To cleanse our hearts of envy, we must identify it as sin and confess it to God. If it persists, we should start praying for the person who we have made the target of our envy. We overcome envy when we can rejoice in the good qualities of others more than we want them for ourselves. The first thing you should keep in mind as you strive to overcome envy is that God wants the best for you.

In other words, it is not God's fault that you think you are missing something. He wanted the best for you because his love for you has no limit. **(Proverbs 27:4, Numbers 5:14).**

PRAYER

Lord Jesus, my sincere desire is to become holy like you. Set me free from anxious thoughts that cause me to become jealous of others. Set my children free of the thoughts that consume their minds which cause jealousy to arise. Substitute the negativity and cruelty within their heart. Lord, I lay their hearts and my desires before you. Search my heart, know my thoughts and see if there is any grievous way in me. Show me where envy has caused me to pursue more over pursuing you. Realign my heart with your will for my life, AMEN.

OVERCOMING FAILURE

SCRIPTURE 58

SCRIPTURE: (Proverbs 24:16 NKJV)

For a righteous man may fall seven times and rise again, but the wicked shall fall by calamity.

DEEPER REFLECTION

He falls seven times- Very often, he finds himself in trouble because his resting place is plundered by the wicked, the thief, the plunderer of the wilderness, who lies in wait for this purpose, **Proverbs 24:15**. But the opposition leads him to the other direction, to get into trouble. And the next verse says the same thing: "Do not rejoice when your enemy falls." The saints of God are destined to "rejoice when they fall into various temptations.

And rises again- Though God allows the hand of violence to mar his tent at times, temptations to assail his mind, and afflictions oppress his body, he constantly emerges; and every time he goes through the oven, he comes out brighter and more refined. **(Psalm 37:24, Psalm 34:19).**

PRAYER

Lord, help us let go of our fear of failure. We know Satan wants to use our fears to hold us back from living boldly for you. Forgive us for not living in faith, and help us from this moment on to live with bold confidence in you, AMEN.

OVERCOMING ADVERSITY

SCRIPTURE 59

SCRIPTURE: (Isaiah 41:13 NKJV)

For I, the LORD your God, will hold your right hand, saying to you, 'Fear not, I will help you.

DEEPER REFLECTION

For the Lord your God will keep your right hand. Take advantage of it, join the league and alliance with your people as it was, we go hand in hand with them; and to have such one with them, and on their side, they need friend not foe: It is expressive of great freedom, familiarity, and friendship, which can assure believers of God's strong affection toward them; and they can conclude themselves, being held by him like a child in the hand of his parents, who then are not afraid of anything. The Lord holds the right hand of His people, teaching them to walk by faith, bringing them into His presence and fellowship with Himself, and keeps them from falling: or, He "will strengthen his right hand" to do the work and service of Him, and oppose the enemies of Him; or He will ease his wishes and fill his hands with His good things. **(Isaiah 43:6, Isaiah 41:10).**

PRAYER

Dear Lord, help me to rest and stand in the Lord's peace. Help me to relax and trust God and let Him fight the invisible spiritual enemy with His peace. For we do not wrestle against flesh and blood, but against principalities, against powers, against the rulers of the darkness of this age, against spiritual hosts of wickedness in the heavenly places, AMEN.

OVERCOMING DISAPPOINTMENT

SCRIPTURE 60

SCRIPTURE: (Jeremiah 29:11 NKJV)

For I know the thoughts that I think toward you, says the LORD, thoughts of peace and not of evil, to give you a future and a hope.

DEEPER REFLECTION

God's thoughts, like those of a father over his loving children, run over his offspring, especially the children of affliction.

To provide you with an expected ending and an expectation - that is, an end to past evils and an expectation of something better in the future **(Isaiah 55:12, Psalm 40:5, Psalm 33:11).**

Every disappointment is a blessing since God has big plans for us and will never let us down. Let us continue to have faith in him.

PRAYER

May You, Lord Jesus, strengthen what's weak in me, comfort me with your peace, and give me wisdom and courage to be patient with this life. Thank you for the promise of full redemption for us and our children. Enable me to launch them on their own journey of faith with the full confidence that You hear our prayers, that You are faithful and that Your redemptive powers reach beyond our years into the generations to come, AMEN.

OVERCOMING TRIALS AND TRIBULATION

SCRIPTURE 61

SCRIPTURE: (John 16:33 NKJV)

These things I have spoken to you, that in me you may have peace. In the world you will have tribulation; but be of good cheer, I have overcome the world.

DEEPER REFLECTION

In the world you will have tribulation- There is no way around it; it is not a paradise, but a purgatory for the saints. It may be compared to the Strait of Magellan, which is said to be a place of that nature, that whichever way a man sets his course, the wind will surely be against him.

I have overcome the world- that is why we are more than conquerors, because we will surely overcome beforehand, **Romans 8:37**. We are winners, **2 Corinthians 2:14**. We do not need to do more, then, like those of Joshua, but to put our feet on the neck of our enemies, already submitted to us by our Jesus.

PRAYER

Lord thank you that through this trial, you are using our lives and circumstances to make a mark on this world. Draw us close to You, please give my children the stamina to handle trials and struggles that come and the faith to endure any hardship. Help them to hear Your voice so many may know of your Great Name, AMEN.

OVERCOMING DEFEAT

SCRIPTURE 62

SCRIPTURE: (Deuteronomy 31:6 NKJV)

Be strong and of good courage, do not fear nor be afraid of them; for the LORD your God, He is the One who goes with you. He will not leave you nor forsake you.

DEEPER REFLECTION

Be strong and of good value. Having shown that God would be with them, by His help, He exhorts the people to be firm and magnanimous. And surely this is a means to confirm our courage, to be sure that the assistance that God promises will suffice for us: so far, it is the case that our zeal and energy to act rightly is affected, by our attribution to the grace of God what foolish men attribute to their own free will. For those who feel aroused by strenuous action depending on their own strength, do nothing but plunge headlong into your mindless recklessness and pride. Let us understand, then, that all exhortations are fleeting and ineffective, that they are based on anything other than simple trust in God's grace.

Considering that, if faith corresponds to the promises of God, and is, as it were, in harmony with them, it must extend to our whole life, even beyond death itself; because God removes all doubt about the future with these words: "I will not leave you nor forsake you."**(Deuteronomy 20:1, 3, 4, Deuteronomy 7:18).**

PRAYER

Powerful Father, thank you that you are my rock and redeemer. I can only fight this fight with You, so please strengthen me so that I can defeat the works of the enemy. God of Power, I will put on the full armor of You, so that I can take my stand against the devil's schemes. In Jesus Name, I pray, AMEN.

OVERCOMING PEER PRESSURE

SCRIPTURE 63

SCRIPTURE: (Exodus 23:2 NKJV)

You shall not follow a crowd to do evil; nor shall you testify in a dispute so as to turn aside after many to pervert justice.

DEEPER REFLECTION

Thou shalt not follow a multitude either their counsel or their example; to do evil – General usage will never excuse us in any ill practice; nor is the broad way ever the safer for its being crowded. We must inquire what we ought to do, not what the most do; because we must be judged by our Master, not our fellow-servants; and it is too great a compliment to be willing to go to hell for company. Neither shalt thou speak in a cause – Either to extenuate or excuse a great fault, aggravate a small one, vindicate an offender, charge guilt on an innocent person, put false glosses or sinister interpretations upon things, or do anything tending to procure an unjust sentence; to decline after many – Either the friends of the party, the judges, the witnesses, or the opinions of the vulgar. **(Exodus 32:1-5, Genesis 7:1).**

PRAYER

Lord, strengthen my children against peer pressure so that they may always stand strong against enticements to do wrong. Bless them and make them fruitful so that their life be struggle-free, toil-free, sorrow-free, hardship-free. We pray a hedge of protection around our child at school, shield them from spiteful remarks, AMEN.

OVERCOMING BULLYING

SCRIPTURE 64

SCRIPTURE: (Romans 2:1 NKJV)

Therefore you are inexcusable, O man, whoever you are who judge, for in whatever you judge another you condemn yourself; for you who judge practice the same things.

DEEPER REFLECTION

The Jews thought of themselves as holy people, entitled to their privileges by right, while they were unthankful, rebellious, and unrighteous. But all who act thus, of every nation, age, and description, must be reminded that the judgment of God will be according to their real character. The case is so plain that we may appeal to the sinner's own thoughts. In every willful sin, there is contempt for the goodness of God. And though the branches of man's disobedience are very various, all spring from the same root. But in true repentance, there must be hatred of former sinfulness, from a change wrought in the state of mind, which disposes of it to choose the good and to refuse the evil. It also shows a sense of inward wretchedness. Such is the great change wrought in repentance; it is conversion, and is needed by every human being. The ruin of sinners is their walking after a hard and impenitent heart. Their sinful doings are expressed by strong words, treasuring up wrath. In the description of the just man, notice the full demand of the law. **(Romans 1:18-20, Romans 2:3).**

PRAYER

I pray that you watch over all of the children who are being bullied today. I pray that you keep them safe from harm and pain, and that you fill their lives with love and joy. When they are being bullied Lord, let them be reminded that they will praise the Lord, who counsels them and in whom they find their identity. Guide them to act swiftly in their defense when they are in danger physically, and compassionately remind them of who they really are when their soul's are under attack. In Jesus Name, AMEN.

OVERCOMING THE DEVIL'S ATTACK

SCRIPTURE 65

SCRIPTURE: (Psalm 18:39 NKJV)

For you have armed me with strength for the battle; you have subdued under me those who rose up against me.

DEEPER REFLECTION

The devil first tries to bring us down by trapping us in sin. If he is successful, he then attempts his accusation. The Bible actually refers to him as "the accuser of the brethren" (**Revelation 12:10).** Satan does not just lead a Christian into sin and leaves him or her to suffer the consequences. He wants the disobedient Christian to be doubly defeated.

"Be strong in the Lord and in the power of His might" **(Ephesians 6:10).** This literally means, "Strengthen yourselves in the Lord." The first thing we must realize is that in our own strength, we are no match for the devil. He is a powerful spiritual being that we must not try to engage on our own.

Satan recognizes that God is your power-base. Therefore, Satan's goal is to get between your soul and God. He tries to separate man's heart from God and inspire man's confidence in himself instead.

PRAYER

Today I bow before you in desperation because, even when I try to think positive thoughts, I am facing continuous attacks by the enemy. Help me Lord to overcome the devil's attack. And as my children face the attack of the enemy, let them be reminded that your grace is sufficient. In Jesus Name, I pray, AMEN.

OVERCOMING LIFE CHALLENGES

SCRIPTURE 66

SCRIPTURE: (Romans 12:21 NKJV)

Do not be overcome by evil, but overcome evil with good.

DEEPER REFLECTION

Truly, nothing is impossible with God **(Luke 1: 37).** No matter what you are dealing with, He will always be there to guide and comfort you **(2 Corinthian 1:3-14).**

The Bible says that Christians are "not of the world," but that doesn't mean that we don't have battles to fight in this world **(John 17:14-15).** In fact, as Christians, we are fighting spiritual battles that others cannot even begin to comprehend.

We are constantly in spiritual warfare with the devil **(Ephesians 6:10-11).** And our flesh is fighting back its old nature **(Galatians 5:16).**

But obstacles aren't necessarily a bad thing! God can use them to grow us up in our faith and teach us how to depend on Him in our everyday lives **(Joshua 1:2-4).**

God never promised us an easy life, but He did promise us

that He will always be there for us **(Israel 41:13).** And never leave us nor forsake us **(Deuteronomy 31:6).**

PRAYER

Father, In Jesus' name, I give you all the struggles of my life today; let the fire of God consume every evil group that stands in my way and my household. O Lord, help me to conquer every difficulty in my life; I declare today that my past faults will no longer impede my progress, I paralyze the devil's attack over my job, my health, my spirit and they will not derail my family's plans, AMEN.

OVERCOMING NON-CHRISTIANS HOLIDAYS

SCRIPTURE 67

SCRIPTURE: (Psalm 27:1)

A Psalm of David. The LORD is my light and my salvation; whom shall I fear? The LORD is the strength of my life; of whom shall I be afraid?

DEEPER REFLECTION

In **(2 Corinthians 6:14–18)**, Paul takes up the question of being mismatched (literally "unequally yoked") with non-Christians. This has implications for both marriage (which is outside our scope here) and working relationships. Up to this point, Paul has vividly portrayed the importance of good relationships with the people with whom we live and work. Paul says in **(1 Cor. 5:9–10)** that we should work with non-Christians, and he discusses how to do so in **(1 Cor. 10:25–33).** See "God's Glory is the Ultimate Goal" **(1 Cor. 10) .**

Here, Paul cautions us about working arrangements with non-believers, invoking a reference to **(Deuteronomy 22:10)** which warns against plowing with an ox and a donkey yoked together. In 2 Corinthians, Paul seems to be talking about a deeper spiritual reality, advising God's people to be wary of yoking with people who serve lawlessness, darkness, idol worship, non christian holidays and Satan himself **(2 Cor. 6:14-15).**

On a general level, Halloween is a time of the year celebrated by advocates of Wicca, a network of practicing witches, Halloween has an overarching associations with death and paganism, which is why it's considered as a non Christian holiday.The Scriptures tell us to put away deeds of darkness **(Rom. 13:12)** and that light has nothing in common with darkness **(2 Cor. 6:14)**. Is celebrating a dark holiday something a child of the light should be doing?

PRAYER

Dear Heavenly Father, You are my sufficiency and strength, my light and my life, my all in all. I pray that when dark clouds of unknowing loom across my children's hearts that I immediately call to mind the wonderful truth of Who You really are. protect us from the darkness of the enemy. Please wipe clean our minds of every evil image, message and content we are exposed to. I reject the darkness and wickedness, and all its associations with evil. In Jesus Christ's Powerful name I pray, AMEN.

BECOMING A ROLE MODEL

SCRIPTURE 68

SCRIPTURE: (Ephesians 6:4 NKJ)

And you, fathers, do not provoke your children to wrath, but bring them up in the training and admonition of the Lord.

DEEPER REFLECTION

Christ put God the Father first in his life and expects us to do the same **(John 5:30).** By myself I can do nothing; I judge only as I hear, and my judgment is just, for I seek not to please myself but Him who sent me.

(Mat 16:24) Then Jesus said to his disciples, "If anyone would come after me, he must deny himself and take up his cross and follow me. This is further exemplified in

(Mat 10:37-38) "Anyone who loves his father or mother more than me is not worthy of me; anyone who loves his son or daughter more than me is not worthy of me, and anyone who does not take his cross and follow me is not worthy of me. It needs to be pointed out that up to this point; Christ had made no mention of his fate, especially because of this non-Jewish mode of capital punishment.

What do we put before Christ and His lifestyle? A job, a reputation, our independence, our vanity, our pride, pleasures? Do we allow our family or job or associates to influence us to disobey God's commandments? Are any of us ashamed to let others know we are Christian? Real role models put ethics above self every time.

PRAYER

Lord Jesus, today, you have become our role model. May we act in the same ways that you do; may your thoughts and may we tell others of your goodness and mercy. Lord, I pray for my children's leadership. Raise them up to be strong leaders in their communities and in their homes. Help them to lead by example, and follow the godly mentorship of others. Fill them with kindness and compassion as they seek to build and encourage those around them, AMEN.

LEADING BY EXAMPLE

SCRIPTURE 69

SCRIPTURE: (1 Timothy 4:12 NKJV)

Let no one despise your youth, but be an example to the believers in word, in conduct, in love, in spirit, in faith, in purity.

DEEPER REFLECTION

Is there any greater example in the entire Bible than Jesus Christ? Certainly not. When Jesus was speaking to His disciples shortly before He was to die on the cross, He told them "I have given you an example that you also should do just as I have done to you. Truly, truly, I say to you, a servant is not greater than his master, nor is a messenger greater than the one who sent him" **(John 13:15-16).** What was it that Jesus had just done? He had just finished washing the disciple's feet! Talk about an example of being a servant. He even washed the feet of the one who would betray Him (Judas). The disciples should have been the ones that had done this in the first place because usually, the one who was the most humble or the lowliest in the home washed the guest's feet...typically a bond-servant. Jesus showed them that even the God-Man could descend to humble Himself to be a servant in the hopes that they should do likewise.

Paul told the Christians in Rome to "Let each of us please his neighbor for his good, to build him up. For Christ did not please himself, but as it is written, 'The reproaches of those who reproached you fell on me'" **(Romans 15:2-3).** So Christ's example showed that He was willing to take the reproaches of men which we deserved, to leave us an example proving that we "have an obligation to bear with the failings of the weak, and not to please ourselves" **(Romans 15:1).**

PRAYER

Everlasting God, kindly assist me in handling my life in a way that will reflect favorably on you. As I bear your worry in my heart, please help me to be compassionate. Allow me to lead by example and inspire others to act honorably and please you in all that they do. Please allow me to serve you and others properly including my children, AMEN.

HAVE THE MIND OF CHRIST

SCRIPTURE 70

SCRIPTURE (Romans 8:9 NKJV)

But you are not in the flesh but in the Spirit, if indeed the Spirit of God dwells in you. Now if anyone does not have the Spirit of Christ, he is not His.

DEEPER REFLECTION

We know we are to bring "every thought into captivity to the obedience of Christ" **(II Corinthians 10:5).** And to "let this mind be in you which was also in Christ Jesus" **(Philippians 2:5).** John tells us "to walk just as He walked" **(I John 2:6).** Peter advises, "Christ . . . [left] us an example, that you should follow His steps" **(I Peter 2:21).**

Spiritually, fidelity is to reproduce faithfully and exactly the thoughts, attitudes, steps, and paths of Jesus Christ. The "sounds" our lives make on earth reach heaven either as the scratchy, tinny, garbled clanging of carnality, or as harmonic, melodious, pleasant reproductions of Christ in us, the hope of glory.

This is where the Pharisees missed the whole point of the

law. They were not like God at all! They were so busy with their little "additions to make it better" that they forgot how to treat each other. This is a great danger facing the church today. We can focus so intently on a specific point of doctrine—the calendar, divorce and remarriage, or church government—that we forget that God bases our judgment on how we treat others **(Matthew 25:34-46).** Christ went about doing well **(Acts 10:38).** He showed compassion, healed, helped, and set a righteous example in all His activities. He never once gossiped, slandered, or verbally abused anyone. While correct teaching is of extreme importance **(II John 10)**, living it is of even greater importance because doers will be justified, not hearers only **(Romans 2:13; James 1:22-25).**

PRAYER

I humbly approach your presence in prayer, seeking the strength and grace of the thought of Christ bestowed upon me by Your Holy Spirit. Give me and my children the fortitude to resist any challenges and temptations that come our way. Lord, shape and form us into a loyal follower of Christ, AMEN.

CHOICE

SCRIPTURE 71

SCRIPTURE: (1 Corinthians 15:33 NKJV)

Do not be deceived: Evil company corrupts good habits.

DEEPER REFLECTION

The variety of translations leaves no room for doubt about the various factors that corrupt good teaching, the good instruction of parents, and the good morals of Christians. Two relevant facts that corrupt the good customs and morals of the Christian are the "good friendships" that the Christian considers he has, that is, friendships with people who do not know Christ as their personal Lord and Savior, people who apparently seem to be good because they are our friendships and many times we are not willing to disappoint those friendships, but we are willing to disappoint Christ, who redeemed us with His blood shed on the cross of Calvary.

It's easier to say... "A little good humor is good from time to time..." it's easier to say... "Not everyone is perfect..." to support a bad behavior. A bad write or a bad talk when we are not willing to accept a timely correction. A little good humor is good from time to time, as long as it does not go against good morals, against good customs, against God's moral principles, but when that "little good humor" violates the moral principles of God, then there is a breaking of the word of God in the life of the Christian.

A verse that goes very well here: **(2 Corinthians 10:5)** casting down arguments and every high thing that exalts itself against the knowledge of God, and bringing every thought captive to the obedience of Christ. Bad company will not only corrupt good morals, but it will also lead the Christian to spiritual and moral failure. Doesn't the Bible imply that the mouth speaks out of the abundance of the heart? That the good man from the good treasure of his heart speaks good things and the bad man from the bad heart speaks bad things?

PRAYER

Holy Father, I beg you this morning to allow us to have our eyes attentive to any stalking of the enemy, that we do not neglect ourselves and begin to be permissive with sin, that we always consider your blessed Word to guide our steps and that we do not seek friendship with the world, and that we do not engage in vain conversations that can lead us to divert our hearts from you giving more importance to other things before you. Allow us today to renew our commitment to you to be faithful to you and keep your Words in our hearts, standing firm and resisting the enemy so that he flees from us. Eternal Father, keep our lives from all temptation and free us from evil, because yours is the kingdom, the power and the glory forever. In the wonderful Name of Jesus Christ, AMEN.

KINDNESS AND COMPASSION

SCRIPTURE 72

SCRIPTURE: (Zechariah 7:9 NKJV)

Thus says the Lord of hosts: Execute true justice, Show mercy and compassion, everyone to his brother.

DEEPER REFLECTION

God's judgments on ancient Israel for their sins were written to warn Christians. The duties required are not to keep fasting and offering sacrifices, but to do so with justice and mercy, tending to the public welfare and loving peace. God's law places a restraint on the heart. But they filled their minds with prejudices against the word of God. Nothing is harder than the heart of a presumptuous sinner. See the fatal consequences of this to his parents. Great sins against the Lord of hosts bring great anger from God's power, which cannot be resisted. Without, if well considered in the heart, it will certainly spoil the success of the prayer. The Lord always hears the cry of the penitent with a broken heart.

PRAYER

Answer me when I call you, my righteous God. Relieve my stress; have mercy on me and listen to my prayers." Lord, like David in Psalms 4, we hail you as our authority and the author of true mercy. Thank you for being a God of compassion and love. Life is hard enough without constantly fearing a God who is present to us. Help us to see what you want us to see when you do not intervene in the consequences of our actions. Help me show it to others when you do. Be that constant voice inside our head and the comforting arms around our heart. Never let me forget to give others the compassion you have shown me, AMEN.

WISDOM

SCRIPTURE 73

CAN THEY MAKE WISE CHOICES IN BAD SITUATIONS?

SCRIPTURE: (Proverbs 4:7 NKJV)

Wisdom is the principal thing; therefore get wisdom. And in all your getting, get understanding.

DEEPER REFLECTION

We must consider our teachers and our parents, although they bring teaching that rebuke and correction, offer them welcome. Solomon's parents loved him, therefore he taught him. Wise and pious men, in all ages of the world, and ranks in society, agree that true wisdom consists in obedience, and is united with happiness. Gain wisdom, and strive for it. Get dominion over your corruptions; have more pains to get this than the wealth of this world. Interest in the salvation of Christ is necessary. This wisdom is the only thing necessary. A soul without true wisdom and grace is a dead soul. How poor, contemptible, and wretched are those who, with all their wealth and power, die without understanding, without Christ, without hope, and without God! Let's pay attention to the words of the One who has words of eternal life. Thus, our path will be smooth before us as we take it, and by keeping the advice, we will avoid being rushed or stumbled.

PRAYER

Lord, teach me to pray, show your purpose in my life and give me the wisdom that comes from you. May my children consistently choose the right and turn away from the wrong. Bless him with wisdom in his choices. And bless him with wisdom concerning whom he chooses for friends. May they mutually encourage each other toward obedience, excellence, and moral character. In the mighty name of Jesus, AMEN.

COMMITMENT

SCRIPTURE 74

SCRIPTURE: (2 Timothy 2:15 NKJV)

Be diligent to present yourself approved to God, a worker who does not need to be ashamed, rightly dividing the word of truth.

DEEPER REFLECTION

This verse of the Scripture should be very significant for those of us who are responsible to give an account to the Great Shepherd of the sheep. God has entrusted us with 66 infallible and errorless books that we must carefully study, allowing the truth of His Word to become part of the very fabric of our being. We must then teach others in the same way **(2 Timothy 2:2**). "My brethren, many of you do not become teachers, knowing that you will receive greater condemnation (judgment)" **(James 3:1).** We certainly must not take this awesome responsibility lightly.

Paul, the wise teacher of Timothy, teaches us, through his letter to his beloved disciple, what it should be: The Duty of a Worker! **(2 Timothy 2:14-16).**

Paul is writing to his beloved disciple, and he is giving him recommendations on what he should do. Let us imagine that it is to us that he is directing these recommendations: Remind them of this... exhorting them... not to contend... which is of no use... Try diligently... as a worker... who uses the word well... avoid profane and vain talk... What a beautiful teaching of the teacher to his beloved student. Paul says: Remind them of these things, charging them in the presence of the Lord, not to fight completely useless verbal battles that confuse the hearers.

When we have been called by the Lord to a ministry, it means that he has chosen us among a lot of people for some very special reason, and this is to serve him as approved workers. This implies that we must be obedient and blameless workers who know the Word and know how to use it.

PRAYER

I recommit my life to you, to love you and follow you, and to be a good example for my kids. I ask that you would show me any areas in my life that need to be changed including any negative tendencies from my family upbringing and how to be freed and healed. Help me to nurture my kids, according to your Kingdom ways and according to their unique characters. I commit to not only teaching, training, and being a Godly example but also to pray & intercede for my kids to become all that you created them to be to give you glory. Holy Spirit, fill me, help me, and guide my steps, AMEN.

STRENGTH

SCRIPTURE 75

SCRIPTURE: (Joshua 1:9 NKJV)

Have I not commanded you? Be strong and of good courage; do not be afraid, nor be dismayed, for the Lord your God is with you wherever you go.

DEEPER REFLECTION

With these words, Jehovah has assured Joshua, His faithful servant, that he could be "strong and courageous" in the face of trials and challenges, no matter how difficult or insurmountable they seemed. Joshua had no reason to be afraid of the future if he obeyed what God commanded him. It would be like having Jehovah right there with him, helping him get ahead. God was with Joshua in that He gave him clear instructions and helped him defeat his enemies.

Where would Joshua get the strength and courage? By that time, Jehovah had already inspired some of the writings in the Bible, and that was surely a great help. Those writings included the Law that Moses, Jehovah's servant, gave to Joshua **(Joshua 1:7).** Speaking of that book of the Law, Jehovah told Joshua: "You must read it and meditate on it day and night" **(Joshua 1:8).** First Joshua had to read and meditate on the Word of God, because that would help him prepare his mind and heart to do the will of Jehovah. And then he had to act according to what he had learned, he had to obey "carefully everything that is written." If he did so, he would make good decisions, and he would do well. And that was just what happened. Although he had to face difficult situations, Joshua lived a full and happy life serving Jehovah **(Joshua 23:14; 24:15).**

PRAYER

Father, strengthen me with Your Spirit and grant me the strength to resist the slingshots of the enemy. May you give my children the strength to do what they need to do each day, that they will be brave as they face the challenges. May my children not fear, for you are with them. As I place my children in your mighty, loving hands, give me peace, knowing that you are right by their side. Please replace their fears with the strength and courage to face whatever the day brings. I ask this in the name of Your Son, AMEN.

SAFETY

SCRIPTURE 76

SCRIPTURE: (Proverbs 18:10 NKJV)

The name of the Lord is a strong tower; the righteous run to it and are safe.

DEEPER REFLECTION

That is, the Lord, as He has revealed Himself in His works, and especially in His word, by His promises, and by the declarations of His infinite perfections, and of His good will to His people; it is a strong tower - it is sufficient for our protection from the greatest dangers. The righteous – by faith and prayer, devotion to God, and dependence on Him; run to Him – as his city of refuge. Having secured their interest in the name of God, they console themselves and benefit: they come out of themselves, withdraw from the world, live above it, dwell in God and God in them, and are secure, as if they were in an impregnable fortress. They think so, and they must think so. Observe, reader, there is enough in God, and in the discoveries He has made of Himself with us, to make us easy at all times. The wealth deposited in this tower is sufficient to enrich us, to be a continual feast and continual treasure for us; the strength of this tower is enough to protect us; the name of the Lord, or that by which He made Himself known both as God and as our God; His titles and attributes; His covenant and all His promises form a tower and a strong tower, impenetrable, impregnable to us, if we are His people. Is this necessary; for they are only the righteous who enter this tower, as it is here stated, or who have access to it, according to **Isaiah 26:2**, which means to defeat the vain confidences of those who, notwithstanding their gross lives of neglect and contempt of God, yet presume to expect His salvation.

God loves you, and gave His son Jesus Christ as a ransom for you **(John 3:16),** even though all human beings are sinners, and this condemns us to eternal death **(Romans 3:23).** The consequence of sin is death, but God offers you a gift, salvation through Jesus **(Romans 6:23).** You can be a child of God, receiving Jesus as your Savior, believing in His name **(John 1:12),** the way to do this is to confess our sins to Him in prayer; He is faithful and just, He will forgive you **(1 John 1:9).** Wait no more, He is knocking on the door of your heart right now, to start a personal relationship with you, which will change your eternity **(Revelation 3:20**) Receive Christ as your Savior today.

PRAYER

Lord, I take a deep breath and prepare to face the struggle of life with all my being, with all my love and with all my creativity, and I do so with confidence and serenity for you are with me. I pray now that You would protect my children as they go throughout their days. Hem them in behind and before and lay Your hand upon them. Lord, I pray for their emotional, physical, and spiritual protection. Keep evil far from them, and help them to trust You, AMEN.

TRUST

SCRIPTURE 77

SCRIPTURE: (Proverbs 3:5-6 NKJV)

Trust in the Lord with all your heart, and lean not on your own understanding; in all your ways acknowledge Him, and He shall direct your paths.

DEEPER REFLECTION

"Trust in Jehovah with all your heart." We show that we trust God when we do things His way. We must trust Him with all our hearts, completely. In the Bible, the word heart is often used to refer to the person we are inside: our emotions, motives, thoughts, and attitudes. Therefore, trusting God with all your heart is more than a feeling; it is a choice we make because we fully believe that our Creator knows what is best for us (**Romans 12:1).** "Lean not on your own understanding." We need to trust God because we cannot depend on our way of seeing things, which is imperfect. If we make decisions independently or are guided only by our feelings, we may make decisions that, although they seem good at first, in the end, they bring us many problems **(Proverbs 14:12; Jeremiah 17:9).** God is much wiser than we are **(Isaiah 55:8, 9).** If we let Him guide us, we will do well in life **(Psalm 1:1-3; Proverbs 2:6-9; 16:20).** "Take Him into account in all your ways." We should take into account what God thinks about the important things in our life; His opinion should also matter to us when making decisions. How do we do it? Praying to Him to ask Him to guide us and follow the advice he gives us in the Bible **(Psalm 25:4; 2 Timothy 3:16, 17).** "He will make your paths straight." God helps us to live according to His righteous standards and thus makes our paths straight **(Proverbs 11:5).** By doing that, we save ourselves a lot of trouble and are much happier **(Psalm 19:7, 8; Isaiah 48:17, 18).**

PRAYER

Today I want to be free and have a confidence similar to that of birds, who do not worry about what they have to eat. I confidently want to leave everything in your hands, Lord, I trust in your protection against all evil, and in your help, I know that you are there even when sometimes it seems that you do not listen to me. I pray that You would enable my children to trust You more and more each day. Prove Yourself to them so they may be convinced beyond a doubt that Your ways are good, AMEN.

FAVOR

SCRIPTURE 78

SCRIPTURE: (Psalm 90:17 NKJV)

And let the beauty of the Lord our God be upon us, and establish the work of our hands for us; Yes, establish the work of our hands.

DEEPER REFLECTION

Those who want to learn true wisdom must pray for divine instruction, must beg to be taught by the Holy Spirit; and for comfort and joy in the returns of God's favor. They pray for God's mercy because they pretend not to claim any merit of their own. His favor would be a fountain full of future joys. It would be a sufficient balance for old pains. May the grace of God in us produce the light of good works. And what divine consolations you gave bring joy in our hearts, and a shine on our faces, and establish the work of our hands. Instead of wasting our precious, fleeting days in pursuit of fantasies, which leave the possessors forever poor, let us seek forgiveness of sins and an inheritance in heaven. Let us pray that the work of the Holy Spirit may appear in the conversion of our hearts, and that the beauty of holiness may be seen in our conduct.

Starting a project with God will never be the same as starting a project without Him. That is why everything we undertake and do must be placed in His wise hands so that His blessing may guide us along the path of victory.

PRAYER

Lord, You are the God of opportunities. Every day, you put in my path opportunities to do well. I pray that I have the courage to respond to the opportunities that come from you. Be a lamp for my children's feet. Be a light to their path. Shine over them. Fill them with your Spirit. Bless them with your favor and peace, AMEN.

DISCERNMENT

SCRIPTURE 79

SCRIPTURE: (Proverbs 3:21-22 NJKV)

My son, let them not depart from your eyes—Keep sound wisdom and discretion. So they will be life to your soul and grace to your neck.

DEEPER REFLECTION

Proverbs chapter 3 is an exhortation of wisdom. God is the source of all wisdom, and when we cling to Him, we receive His guidance and direction from Him for everything we should do or say. That attitude inspires us to have good judgment, to act with prudence and discretion. The prudent person fixes his eyes on Jesus and seeks in Him the necessary wisdom for each moment. He allows true life, which springs from a personal relationship with God, to flow through Him, adorning everything He does or says. This is how he brings blessing and encouragement to those he meets on his path.

We do not suffer the words of Christ to depart from us, but we maintain prudence and discretion; then, let us walk safely in his ways. Natural life, and all that pertains to it, will be under the protection of God's providence; spiritual life, and all his interests, under the protection of His grace, so that they will be kept from falling into sin or trouble.

The Bible advises: "Safeguard practical wisdom and thinking ability." And it also indicates the result of doing so: "Then you will walk safely on your way, and not even your foot will strike anything" **(Prov. 3:21, 23).** Therefore, knowing what practical wisdom is and how it is demonstrated protects us. It helps us not to stumble spiritually and gives us stability.

PRAYER

Lord, I ask you to give me a discerning Spirit so that I can make the right decisions at all times, that even when your instructions seem foolish, I will obey them, knowing that they will help me to live directly in the center of your will in the name of Jesus. Give my children alertness, spiritual discernment, wisdom to avoid temptation and to make the best choices. I thank you that my children will gain knowledge, wisdom, and discernment through your Word, AMEN.

LOVE

SCRIPTURE 80

SCRIPTURE: (1 John 4:16 NJKV)

And we have known and believed the love that God has for us. God is love, and he who abides in love abides in God, and God in him.

DEEPER REFLECTION

Perhaps **1 John 4:16** is the verse of all verses that encapsulates the very essence of God and His plan of redemption. Perhaps this is the truth that helps us understand who God is, what He has done for us, what He is doing and what He will continue to do, in and through all who believe in the name of the only begotten Son of God and put their trust in Him. And we have known and believed the love that God has for us. God is love; and he who remains in love remains in God, and God in him. **(1 John 4:16 KJV)**

John had a very special relationship with Jesus. He often referred to himself as the apostle whom Jesus loved. When John wrote this letter, love was the main thing he wanted to write about; it was the main thing he wanted the church to understand. That's because it is the most important part of our relationship with God and is the central theme of **1 John 4:16**. God was never meant to be our religion; it was our hearts from the beginning that drew us into a relationship with Him. How we view God has a lot to do with how we approach Him. God loves us like a father loves his own son. He has given us the Spirit of adoption by which we call Him, Abba, father!

The love of God is the cross of Jesus, and through His cross, a man or woman can receive God's forgiveness. It was God's love that sent Jesus Christ to the cross. No matter how terrible our sins are, God loves us and that is a truth that we should not question. I want to invite you to put into practice the verse **1 John 4:16**, and that you remain in love every day; in this way, God will remain in us.

PRAYER

Loving Father, I praise You for Your heart of love that is open towards me, and for the many ways that You shower Your love into my life. Use me I pray, to stream Your gracious love through my life out to the weary and thirsty souls that You place in my path. Lord, I pray that my children will love you with all their heart, soul, mind, and strength. May this command govern their lives each day. As they seek to love you, may they also love their neighbor, and grow in compassion and kindness towards those around them. May the love of Christ shine brightly in their lives as they seek to serve you each day. This I ask in Christ's name and for His greater glory, AMEN.

FAITH

SCRIPTURE 81

SCRIPTURE: (Hebrews 11:1 NKJV)

Now faith is [the] substance of things hoped for, the evidence of things not seen.

DEEPER REFLECTION

"Faith is the certainty that what is expected will happen." In the original text of **Hebrews 11:1**, the Greek word used for "faith" conveys the idea of security, confidence, and firm conviction. That faith is not based on mere wishful thinking; that faith is "the certainty that what is expected will happen." The Greek word that is translated, "certainty that it will happen," could also be translated as "property deed". A deed is a guarantee that gives security or confidence to the person who has it. "Faith is . . . the convincing proof [or "obvious demonstration," note] that there are unseen realities." Faith is born when you have solid evidence. These tests are so strong that they convince the person that something is real, even if he cannot see it. The biblical book of Hebrews is a letter that Apostle Paul wrote to first-century Christians who lived in and around Jerusalem. In this part of the letter, Paul talks about how important faith is. For example, he says, "***Without faith it is impossible to please God, because whoever comes to God must believe that he exists and that he rewards those who diligently seek him***" **(Hebrews 11:6).** After defining what faith is in **Hebrews 11:1**, Paul gives examples of men and women from Bible times who demonstrated that quality. He says that they demonstrated their faith by acting according to God's will **(Hebrews 11:4-38).**

PRAYER

Loving Father, I can be so entrenched in my own thinking that sometimes I doubt Your Word and question Your promises, often wishing I had some concrete proof of Your love for me. And yet Your Word and Promises are sure and Your faithfulness stretches beyond the limits of time and space. Thank You for the gift of faith, and I pray that day by day, my loving trust in You and the reality of Your Word will become increasingly established within my heart – for I long to please You in all I say and do. I ask that you would strengthen my children's faith each day. May they not waver on the waves of doubt and uncertainty, but may they know with assurance that you are with them. Help them to diligently spend time in your Word, seeking your face for direction and guidance. May their faith grow each day as they trust in you. In Jesus' name I pray, AMEN.

PURITY

SCRIPTURE 82

SCRIPTURE: (Matthew 5:8)

Blessed are the pure in heart, for they shall see God.

DEEPER REFLECTION

Being blessed is a state of well-being or happiness in a relationship with God. The pure in heart are happy because their sin has been forgiven, and they have been granted access to God the Father. In our culture, the word "blessed" often refers to receiving immeasurable wealth, material goods, or fame. But in the kingdom of God, "being blessed" refers to our satisfaction in God and the joy of our salvation. King David demonstrates this truth by understanding the weight of sin and calling for renewed delight in God's salvation: ***"Let me hear joy and gladness; let the bones you have broken rejoice. Hide your face from my sins and erase all my iniquities. Create in me a clean heart, O God, and renew a right spirit within me. Do not cast me out of your presence, and do not take away your Holy Spirit. Restore to me the joy of your salvation, and sustain me with a willing spirit.***"- **(Psalm 51:8-12).** David accepts that when his sins are hidden from the face of God, joy and gladness are found in the midst of brokenness. He has made the connection that a pure heart and spirit restore joy. If we have put our faith in the gospel, then our sins are covered by the blood of Jesus, and our lives are hidden in Christ **(Colossians 3:17, Ephesians 1:7).**

PRAYER

Heavenly Father, thank You that my heart has been cleansed of sin through faith in the Lord Jesus Christ, my God and Savior. Keep me low at the Cross and broken before You, and open my eyes to see more and more of Your beauty and grace, and I pray that may I live to Your praise and glory. Lord, I ask today that you will guard my children's purity by helping them live according to your Word. Help them not to conform to the patterns of this world, but to daily conform to your truth by the renewing of their minds. This I ask in Jesus' name, AMEN.

SPEECH

SCRIPTURE 83

SCRIPTURE: (Ephesians 4:29 NKJV)

Let no corrupt word proceed out of your mouth, but what is good for necessary edification, that it may impart grace to the hearers.

DEEPER REFLECTION

Jehovah is the source of *"every good gift and every perfect gift"* **(James 1:17)**. For example, he has given us something that distinguishes us from animals and that allows us to express our ideas and feelings: the faculty of speech. But this gift, like the comparison car, can be misused. In fact, many people use it irresponsibly and harm others. Do we understand, then, how disappointed Jehovah must be?

If we want to stay in God's love, we have to use this gift as he wants. Or we have to follow the instructions that he has left in the Bible: "***Do not proceed from your mouth any corrupt saying, but everything that is good for the edification [of the neighbor] according to need, so that it imparts whatever is favorable to the hearers"* (Ephesians 4:29)**. Therefore, next we will examine what kind of language we should avoid and how we can use the gift of speech to edify our fellow human beings. But, first of all, let's see why it is so important to control the tongue. The first reason to control ourselves when speaking is the great power of words. Proverbs 15:4 alludes to this power: "***The calmness of the tongue is a tree of life, but the crookedness of it means a breaking of the spirit.***" * The calm words of a kind tongue are as refreshing as dew and as comforting as balm. Instead, the malicious comments of a wicked tongue crush anyone's spirits. As we see, words can hurt, or they can heal **(Proverbs 18:21).**

PRAYER

Heavenly Father, I pray that no unwholesome words would proceed from my mouth, but that the words of my lips and the meditation of my heart may be gracious and good. I pray that my speech will edify my brothers and sisters in Christ and honor Your name by speaking the truth in love. Today, I ask You for godly, loyal friends for my children. Friends who are pure in heart, and gracious in speech. This I ask in Jesus' name, AMEN.

CONDUCT

SCRIPTURE 84

SCRIPTURE: (Proverbs 22:6 NJKV)

Train up a child in the way he should go, and when he is old he will not depart from it.

DEEPER REFLECTION

The relationship that parents have with God can be the model that children follow. If children never see parents praying or reading the Bible, they will not understand its importance. Many families decide to have a time of prayer and reading of the Word each week (family altar). This is a good idea if done with love and understanding, keeping in mind that children are not going to be quiet and still for long. It can be just 10 or 15 minutes of talking about a Bible story, singing, and praying together as a family. It is during these fun times of family worship that many children decide to give their lives to the Lord. What a blessing for parents! Being channels of blessing for children, guiding them with love towards Jesus, is the most precious task they can do. ***"Nothing brings me more joy than hearing that my children practice the truth"*** **(3 John 1:4).** It is important to remember that

Proverbs 22:6 is not a promise to parents. The children will have to decide for themselves whether they want to serve God or not. The important thing is that parents fulfill their responsibility by providing the child with the best compass: the opportunity to cultivate a personal relationship with God. That intimate and direct relationship with the heavenly Father will make a difference.

PRAYER

Heavenly Father, thank You for the privilege, responsibility, and joy of the children You have placed in my life. I humbly ask that You would guide me in the way that I should teach them and train them and pray that they may grow up in the fear and nurture of the Lord. May they grow in godly conduct, make wise choices and learn to be both responsible towards others and accountable to authority. Keep them from worldly ways, direct and govern their lives, and may they never depart from the way of righteousness, in Jesus' name I pray, AMEN.

OBEDIENCE

SCRIPTURE 85

SCRIPTURE: (1 Samuel 15:22 NJKV)

Has the Lord as great delight in burnt offerings and sacrifices, as in obeying the voice of the Lord? Behold, to obey is better than sacrifice, and to heed than the fat of rams.

DEEP REFLECTION

God will bless your obedience always, engrave yourself on fire, that God blesses your obedience and not your intentions, look for his direction in the word and follow it to the letter, you have his direction clear through it and through His Holy Spirit. He is good at forgiving if we repent, but let us not get used to this "I do what I want and then I ask for forgiveness, totally He forgives me", because God knows our hearts and our intentions, says the word, and yes, He will forgive, but we cannot enjoy His blessings if we act like this. We cannot "wet the ear of the Lord", as the saying goes, because He scrutinizes our hearts and thoughts. Saul wanted to pretend that nothing had happened, and said, I do this and then I give him an offering, but for God, the best of our offerings is our obedience.

Has it happened to you that your heart hurts after you realize that you have sinned in something? It is that when we know the great sacrifice that Jesus made for us, and that this sacrifice was to take away the sin, and that we were forgiven, then we understand that when I obstinately sin, it is a sign that I do not care about that sacrifice. And when we realize this, then we react, but if we react, please, let's not repeat it. Let's remember that Jesus forgave Mary Magdalene of her sin, and told her, "don't worry, I don't even condemn you, go and sin no more." Let's not open the door to the enemy with disobedience because this makes us fall into a curse.

PRAYER

Heavenly Father, thank You for the many lessons that I can learn from the history of the people and kings of Israel. Help me to listen to Your voice and pay heed to Your Word, for it is my desire to honor You in thought, word, deed, and motive, through the power of the indwelling Holy Spirit. Teach my children the powerful gift and blessing of obedience. Help them to understand that when they obey us as their parents, they are truly obeying and submitting to you. Help them to honor you by walking in obedience to you, and may they live long, fulfilled lives in service to you. This I ask in Jesus' name, AMEN.

THANKFULNESS

SCRIPTURE 86

SCRIPTURE: (1 Thess. 5:16-18 NKJV)

Rejoice always, pray without ceasing, and in everything give thanks; for this is the will of God in Christ Jesus for you.

DEEPER REFLECTION

Paul writes this letter to the Thessalonians and among the final instructions are these, God wants us to always be joyful. I know that sometimes it is difficult to be joyful when we find ourselves in health tests or financial difficulties or with problems in our family but still; Paul reminds us that it is God's will; He commands us to be joyful... a verse that encourages me right now is **Romans 8: 18** where it says that nothing we suffer here compares to the glory to come. So I am sure that all suffering, however hard it may be; must have an end and that one day I will be in glory with our Lord. He also commands us to pray without ceasing, and I want to tell you that I am a person who easily loses focus, but I ask God to help me stay focused by praying for the needs of our church, for the health needs of some people I know and appreciate and for each one of the things that

God puts on my heart without stopping praying for them until God answers that prayer because I know that God has the power to answer each one of them, according to His good will. Giving thanks to God in every situation- this is equally difficult when we go through hard situations, but we know that if God has allowed it, it always has a purpose for our life, and after the test, we will be better children of God. So let's not forget to show that joy to the cloud of witnesses that surround us, this bears good witness to God and glorifies Him.

Let's not forget to pray for our needs and those of others. It is important to accompany our brothers who are in trials just as we would like them to accompany us in our difficulties. Let us always be grateful, we are children of an eternal King, and we will reign with Him always.

PRAYER

Heavenly Father, I praise Your holy name for all Your goodness and loving-kindness to me and to all mankind. Thank You for sending Your Son to be our Kinsman-Redeemer. All praise to Your name from this day forth and forevermore. Thank you for my children. Bless them with your love and peace, Protect them with your truth and strength, Engage them with your hope and vision. May they rejoice always and grow into mighty prayer warriors, praying always with thankful hearts. In Jesus' name, AMEN.

PEACE

SCRIPTURE 87

SCRIPTURE: (John 14:27 NJKV)

Peace I leave with you, my peace I give to you; not as the world gives do I give to you. Let not your heart be troubled, neither let it be afraid.

DEEPER REFLECTION

Shalom was a Hebrew declaration that expressed the true desire of the one who desired it for a life full of security, prosperity, health, and satisfaction, and in this way, God asked the priests to be the ones who, with their lips, declared it to the Israelites: ***"Speak to Aaron and his sons and tell them: Thus you shall bless the children of Israel, saying to them: The Lord bless you and keep you; Jehovah make his face shine upon you, and be gracious to you; The LORD lift up his countenance upon you, and give you peace.",*** **(Numbers 6:23-26)**. These verses are known as the priestly prayer, and in them, we can see God's desire to wish His people true peace. If we review this sentence, we will see that the consequence of a life in peace is the product of receiving God's blessing, his divine protection, of finding thanks in His eyes and reaching his mercy. Now we see Christ, as the true and only High Priest, proclaiming with his own lips the peace of God: Peace I leave with you, my peace I give to you. Christ's desire is to bring peace to the hearts of men, and the truth is that only He can bring it because it is through His saving work that this occurs, which is why apostle Paul teaches us that one of the results of justification is peace: ***"Therefore having been justified by faith, we have peace with God through our Lord Jesus Christ"*** **(Romans 5:1)**. When Christ forgives our sins, His blood cleanses us from all sins in such a way that enmity that existed between us and God disappears, since what separated us were our sins, but now by His grace, we have been reconciled, and if reconciled, blessed by God and incorporated into a new life full of hope and joy, and this is peace.

PRAYER

Loving Father, thank You that I have peace with You. Thank You, Father, that Christ is my Peace. Lord, I ask that you will flood my children with peace in their hearts that surpasses all understanding. You say that our hearts will be kept in perfect peace when our minds are focused on you (Isaiah 26:3). Help them to remember that they can call on you when they are in need of peace and rest for their weary souls. In His name I pray, AMEN.

PATIENCE

SCRIPTURE 88

SCRIPTURE: (Romans 2:4 NKJV)

Or do you despise the riches of His goodness, forbearance, and long-suffering, not knowing that the goodness of God leads you to repentance?

DEEPER REFLECTION

Paul expresses God's attitude toward us as he waits for us to stop rebelling against His will: "kindness, forbearance, and patience." Now we are told that the realization of how much God loves us should lead us to repentance. Or rather, "Because you have mistaken God's kindness and patience for impotence and indifference, you have failed to see the need for repentance from Him." Which one is for you? What draws you to God, the threat of punishment or the love of him?

In temporary things- You, perhaps, have been prospered above your peers. God has granted you wealth and health. You are happy with your wife and children. A thousand evils you have been saved from. In spiritual things- You are in the very focus of the Christian light. The Word of God is on your table;

you hear the fervent preaching of the gospel. A tender conscience makes your path to perdition peculiarly difficult. The Spirit has wrestled with you so much that, at times, you almost fell into the Savior's arms. He has been patient and suffered for your sins. Patience has to do with the magnitude of sin; long-suffering with the multiplicity of it. Many have been snatched from vice only to return to its deep ditch of filth. They have trembled on the verge of death, but God has allowed them to regain strength. They despise His love, but He perseveres in it.

PRAYER

Father, thank you for Your grace and patience towards me.When my children test me, teach me, God, how to respond with wisdom. When I grow irritable, send me patience. When my fury rages, teach me the power of restraint. Continue to draw me back once again into Your sweet arms of comfort so I can enjoy gracious fellowship with You. This I pray In Jesus' name, AMEN.

JOY

SCRIPTURE 89

SCRIPTURE: (Psalm 30:5 NKJV)

For His anger is but for a moment, his favor is for life; weeping may endure for a night, but joy comes in the morning.

DEEPER REFLECTION

The great things the Lord has done for us, both by His providence and by His grace, unite us in gratitude to do everything possible to advance His kingdom among men, although the most we can do is very little. . The saints of God in heaven sing to Him; why shouldn't those on earth do the same? Not one of the perfections of God all bears in it more terror to the wicked, or more comfort to the godly, than His holiness. It is a good sign that we are in some measure partakers of His holiness if we can gladly rejoice at the memory of it. Our happiness is bound up in divine favor; if we have to, we have enough, whatever we want; but as long as the wrath of God continues, always crying of the saints continues.

Our natural life is favored by God. In Him we live, move, and have our being; He protects us from innumerable evils; He gives us bread, water, clothing, health, strength, and intelligence. Our spiritual life is favored by God. Our eternal life is from the favor of God. By that favor, we become entitled to heaven through the merits and justice of Christ; by that favor, we are gathered to heaven through regeneration and sanctification; by that favor, we are taken to heaven, through all the difficult pilgrimage of life. Oh, what views will the spirit redeemed from the favor of God have!

PRAYER

Heavenly Father, I praise and thank You for Your loving-kindness and long-suffering toward me and all Your children. Thank You that no matter what difficulty and pain I may go through in this life, help me to remember that weeping will be replaced with laughter, and pain with joy. I pray for my children happiness, that they see the joy in the little things all around them. I pray that their joy is infectious and that they share it with as many people as possible.In Jesus' name, AMEN.

SUCCESS

SCRIPTURE 90

SCRIPTURE: (Joshua 1:8 NKJV)

This Book of the Law shall not depart from your mouth, but you shall meditate in it day and night, that you may observe to do according to all that is written in it. For then you will make your way prosperous, and then you will have good success.

DEEPER REFLECTION

When God told Joshua that the Israelites would take possession of the Promised Land, He included a very important command: meditate on His law at all times, and obey everything it says. These would guarantee them success. Meditation on the Word remains crucial for Christians today. In our culture, we are inundated with worldly values and priorities that shut out God, and unless we guard our hearts, we will begin to accept them.

We must remember that the prosperity and success that the Lord spoke of is prosperity and success in the eyes of God and not necessarily in the eyes of the world. From a New Testament perspective, we know that the main application of this promise would be eternal riches and Christ-centered success, soul prosperity, and spiritual success (although some measure of success by our human effort will generally also occur when we live according to the wisdom of God). However, with this caveat, let us not lose sight of the relationship between meditation on God's Word and true success. True success is promised to those who meditate on the Word of God, who think deeply about the scriptures not just once a day, but at times throughout the day and night. They meditate so much that the Scriptures saturate their conversation. The fruit of your meditation is action. They do what they find written in the Word of God, and as a consequence, God makes their way prosperous and grants them success. Why? Because striving to "obey all that is written there" in God's Word is just one of the biblical ways of describing what the New Testament would characterize as seeking Christlikeness, and God loves to bless conformity to His Son. From eternity past, God predestined all who are His to become like Christ **(see Romans 8:29).** For all future eternity, all who are in Christ will be glorified **(see Romans 8:30)**, that is, "we will be like him" **(1 John 3:2):** sinless people, perfect, reflecting the glory of God forever. So, during our earthly pilgrimage, the more we obey the Word of God, the more we become like Christ, the more we fulfill God's eternal plan to make us like His Son. That's why God loves to bless obedience. Just as meditation leads to obedience, obedience results from God's blessing. We are not told how much of that blessing is material and how much is spiritual, or how much of that blessing is in this world and how much is in the next, but we do know that God does bless obedience.

PRAYER

Loving Lord, thank You for the Scriptures. I pray that in the weeks and months that lie ahead, I may read, mark, learn, and inwardly digest Your Word and treasure it in my heart, for I desire to prosper in the things of God and to give glory to Your name. I pray for Your favor that success may follow my children, I pray that You will grant them the desires of their hearts so that they can flourish and be successful according to your will. In Jesus' name, AMEN.

PROVISION

SCRIPTURE 91

SCRIPTURE: (Phil 4:19 NKJV)

And my God shall supply all your need according to His riches in glory by Christ Jesus.

DEEPER REFLECTION

It is necessary to take into account at all times the verse **Philippians 4:19** of the Holy Bible in order to reflect on it. Surely it would be appropriate to ask ourselves, what did God our Lord want to propose to us with the verse **Philippians 4:19**?

Without a doubt, one of the texts preferred by the people of God is the one that Paul mentions in this final part of his epistle of joy: ***"My God will supply all your needs according to His riches in glory in Christ Jesus"*** **Philippians 4:14-20**

A promise like this is very encouraging, especially when we see that there are stormy winds that are hitting the livelihood of the family very hard. It is also encouraging when we see that the appearance of a disease is present to frighten us and rob us of the joy that comes from the Lord. And it is also when we notice that there are gaps in life, such as: loneliness, lack of understanding, and in some cases, even the lack of true love. It is good that we can lay hold of this promise, for all things are possible according to "His riches in glory in Christ Jesus." However, we could not take this text out of its context to give it a free interpretation. Paul affirmed this promise after having acknowledged and praised the Philippians' involvement in his ministry. When he could move about preaching, he said: ***"Before you know that for what has been necessary for me and those who are with me, these hands have served me..."*** **(Acts 20:34).** But now he is in prison, and he needed to depend on others, among whom the Philippians appear, the most faithful in the matter of "give and receive."

PRAYER

Father, thank you for all that you have given me and all that you will give me. You have not only supplied all my needs, but you have given my children untold riches in Christ. Help me to live as one so blessed that I can say with Paul, my God shall supply all your need according to His riches to the glory of Him in Christ Jesus, AMEN.

DISCIPLINE

SCRIPTURE 92

SCRIPTURE: (Hebrews 12:8 NKJV)

But if you are without chastening, of which all have become partakers, then you are illegitimate and not sons.

DEEPER REFLECTION

The persevering obedience of faith in Christ, the race before the Hebrews was created, in which they must either win the crown of glory, or have eternal misery on their part; and is ahead. By the sin that besets us, understand that the sin to which we are most prone, or to which we are most exposed, by habit, age, or circumstances. This is a most important exhortation; for as long as a man's darling sin, whatever it may be, remains subdued, it will prevent him from running the Christian race, since it takes from him all motives for running, and gives power to all discouragement. When tired and weak in their minds, make them remember that the holy Jesus suffered to save them from eternal misery. By fixing our eyes on Jesus, the thoughts of Him would strengthen holy affections, and will subject him to his carnal desires. Let's see then, we consider it frequently. What are our little rehearsals to their agonies, or even to our deserts? What are the sufferings of many others? There is a propensity in believers to grow weary and faint under trials and afflictions; this is from the imperfection of grace and the remains of corruption. Christians must not faint under their trials. Though his enemies and persecutors may be instruments of inflicting suffering, yet they are divine punishments; his heavenly Father has His hand in everything, and in the end knew that He will answer for everyone. They must not do in the light of afflictions, and be unfeeling under them, for they are the hand and the rod of God, and they are his rebukes for sin. They must not be discouraged and sink under trials, nor worry and complain, but you have to have faith and patience. God may let other people alone in his sins, but he will correct the sin in His own children. In this, he acts as He has become his father. Our earthly parents may sometimes punish us, to satisfy his passion, instead of reforming our ways. But the Father of our souls never grieves Himself or His children voluntarily. He is always for our benefit. Our whole life here is a state of infancy, and imperfect to spiritual things; therefore, we have to submit to the discipline of such a state. When we reach a perfect state, we will be fully reconciled to God's punishment of all of us now. God's correction is not condemnation; punishment will be borne with patience, and greatly promote holiness.

PRAYER

Lord, guide me daily and give me the discipline to study your word, make time for relationship with you, and actively, purposefully teach my children how their lives can be used to glorify you in word and deed. Help them to hear Your voice behind them and to blindly obey In the name above all names, Jesus Christ, AMEN.

UNDERSTANDING

SCRIPTURE 93

SCRIPTURE: (Proverbs 4:7 NKJV)

Wisdom is the principal thing; therefore get wisdom. And in all your getting, get understanding.

DEEPER REFLECTION

King Solomon asked God for wisdom above all else, being able to ask for riches or power as any simple mortal would. The Lord granted it to him to the point that there was no wiser king before or after him. In the midst of trials, the first request we make to God should be for wisdom; to understand His purpose, to discern what is convenient to do, and thus make the right decisions in accordance with His will.

Just as the body and mind need nourishment, so does the spirit. I plead with the youth: Acquire knowledge, seek and develop knowledge of the spirit, seek knowledge of the mind, seek knowledge of the soul, and be refined men and women, wise in every way, for I testify before you this day that security, true security, is based on the knowledge of the divinity of Jesus Christ. This is the beginning of all learning and all wisdom. This is the greatest knowledge, the greatest understanding, the greatest consolation that men can have. If men have this knowledge in their hearts, they can meet all the vicissitudes of life.

PRAYER

Lord, teach me to pray, show Your purpose in my life and give me the wisdom and understanding that comes from You. Help my children understand the power of prayer and its effect in their lives. In the mighty name of Jesus, AMEN.

CREATIVITY

SCRIPTURE 94

SCRIPTURE: (Proverbs 22:29 NJKV)

Do you see a man who excels in his work? He will stand before kings; He will not stand before unknown men.

DEEPER REFLECTION

Curiously, these situations abound, many workers go through changing jobs or complaining that they are not recognized or valued; the Bible teaches us many principles that we must follow so that we can do well at work; here is one of them. **(Proverbs 22:29)** ***"Have you seen a man diligent in his work? He will stand before kings; He will not stand before the lowly."*** The word diligent means to be diligent and helpful. We cannot be ignored by our Bosses when we are diligent and helpful. Sometimes we are afraid of being that way because of what others will say, and since they are going to brand us as barbers, obviously, we must be helpful but not servile.

A person who is diligent and helpful, commonly called restrained, is a person who is attentive to the needs of his boss and his colleagues, but also collaborates to satisfy them. If he sees that papers have fallen from a desk, he goes and helps to pick them up; if the coffee spilled, he immediately looks for something to clean up, not because it is his job but because he is needed to solve a problem. By being attentive, someone will see you and recognize you, if it is not your boss, someone else will want you to work for him and you will have a better position. In **Proverbs 22:29**, he makes an affirmation, therefore it is a fact that it will happen if you believe it and fulfill the condition. Decide to be diligent today to lay the foundations of your tomorrow, leave the complaints, criticism and resentments, and apply yourself to change your work status by being diligent and helpful. God bless you.

PRAYER

Dear Heavenly Father, thank you for making us in your image. Let your creative power surge through us today. Father pour out ideas and insight; help us to respond to life's challenges with an ease. Let your light shine in us. Grant us the skill, intelligence, knowledge and craftsmanship to devise artistic designs with Kingdom excellence. In Jesus Name I pray, Amen.

LEADERSHIP

SCRIPTURE 95

SCRIPTURE: (Deuteronomy 28:13 NJKV)

And the Lord will make you the head and not the tail; you shall be above only, and not be beneath, if you heed the commandments of the Lord your God, which I command you today, and are careful to observe them.

DEEPER REFLECTION

And you will always receive these blessings: "God will bless you wherever you live, be it in the country or in the city. "God will bless his children, and his crops and cattle. "God will bless you in your homes, in your travels, and in everything you do. They will always be very happy in the country that God will give them. They will never lack food and will always have bread on the table. "God will give you victory over your enemies. Armies may come against you in battle array, but they will have to flee in complete disorder. "If you obey God in everything, he will fulfill His promise and you will be His special people. Then all the people will see that you are a son of God, and they will be afraid of you. "When you are in the land that God promised to give your ancestors, He will treat you kindly. He will allow them to have many children, and He will cause his herds to multiply. "Whatever you sow will produce bountiful crops, for God will open the heavens, where He keeps the rain, and water your crops. In everything you do, it will always go well for you. They will never have to borrow anything; on the contrary, you will have plenty to lend to other countries. "If you obey God's commandments and never disobey God or worship false gods, you will always be the greatest country in the world.

This chapter is a great exposition of two words, the blessing and the curse. They are real things and have real effects. The blessings are here put before the curses. God is slow to anger, but quick to show mercy. It is His joy to bless. It is better that we be drawn to what is good by a childlike hope of God's favor, than we are frightened of it by a slavish fear of its wrath. The blessing is promised, on the condition that they diligently listen to the voice of God. Let them keep up to religion, the form and power of it, in their families and the nation, then God's providence would prosper all their external concerns.

PRAYER

God teach me to steward well the talents entrusted to me. Let me not be like the one who buried his talents; show me instead how to multiply them and bless others so I can lead better. Help me to raise my children as leaders so that they remain pure and unblemished throughout their lives, and when we have finished our journey, we pray that You take us into Your heavenly kingdom. In the name of our Redeemer, so be it, AMEN.

PROTECTION

SCRIPTURE 96

SCRIPTURE: (2 Thessalonians 3:3 NKJV)

But the Lord is faithful, who will establish you and guard you from the evil one.

DEEPER REFLECTION

The same God who wants to save us and who can save us, can also sustain us and can protect us. The Lord does not do His work halfway or in part. Actually, He saves us for a purpose and the moment of our salvation is nothing more than the beginning of what He wants with us. Something that will be fully realized at the coming of our Lord Jesus Christ.

***"Faithful is he who calls you, and he also will do it."* (1 Thessalonians 5:24)**. In the difficulties of this life, there is no reason to be discouraged, nor to be frustrated, nor to throw in the towel, knowing in whom we have believed. In the midst of tribulations, persecutions or temptations... He is faithful. ***"So that those who suffer according to the will of God, commend their souls to the faithful Creator, and do well."* (1 Peter 4:19).**

"Let us hold fast, without wavering, the profession of our hope, because faithful is he who promised." **(Hebrews 10:23)**

"No temptation has overtaken you that is not human; but faithful is God, who will not let you be tempted beyond what you can bear, but he will also provide a way out with the temptation, so that you can endure." **(1 Corinthians 10:13)**

If we fail him, if we go astray or if we deny him (as Peter did), there is hope because He is faithful. He knows our weaknesses, and He knows our statement: *"Wretched me! Who will deliver me from this body of death?"* **as Paul wrote in (Romans 7:24).**

"If we confess our sins, he is faithful and just to forgive us our sins, and to cleanse us from all unrighteousness." **(1 John 1:9)**

What tranquility surrounds us when we recognize in whose hand we are truly at the moment of being saved? No wonder Paul could say in **Romans 8:38-39**, "Therefore I am sure that... (Nothing)...shall be able to separate us from the love of God, which is in Christ Jesus our Lord."

PRAYER

Dear Heavenly Father, today I ask for your protection over our children. Let no trouble fall on them today. Keep them away from accidents. Allow no evil to influence their hearts. Cover them with the precious blood of Christ. Take charge over them so that they do not strike their foot against a stone. In Jesus Christ, in whose name I pray, AMEN.

HONOR

SCRIPTURE 97

SCRIPTURE: (Romans 12:10 NJKV)

Be kindly affectionate to one another with brotherly love, in honor giving preference to one another.

DEEPER REFLECTION

God tells us to love, respect, and honor each other. Another person talks about the importance of respect, and we turn to what he said, leaving aside the words that God gave us two thousand years ago. Why downplay the word of the Lord? Why give more credit to our contemporaries? On the other hand, we have a commandment to follow today: love one another. Not only respect or tolerate but love. Hard. Very difficult. God gives us no room to "maneuver." There is no way to make excuses. There are no excuses. The Lord practically has us cornered. He wants us to love each other. And that love is not what we want or think it should be. It must be with brotherly love, respect and honor. Who are you addressing in this way? Personally not many people. In fact, with one hand, I probably have fingers left over... It is not about thinking of this commandment as it suits us, but rather we must accommodate ourselves to it. We must transform our thoughts, our pride, our selfishness, and our dedication. Perhaps it is easier for you to respect, but it is difficult for you to love and give honor or any variant of these premises. The important thing is to understand that God is asking us all! If you really want to give your life to God, you must love your neighbor as He established it and not as you think it should be done: brotherly love, respect and honor.

This is a call from God to "filter" those who follow Him to receive and those who want and seek to serve Him. What side are you on? Jesus left us His clear example of His coming: I came to serve and not to be served. Do you want to be served or are you willing to serve by giving yourself to God and loving your neighbor with brotherly love, respect and honor?

PRAYER

Loving Father, please let your blessings and Word shine on my children and family, as we seek to honor you. I pray that they find security and confidence fully in you, knowing that you are trustworthy, true and honorable. In Jesus' Name, AMEN.

COMMON SENSE & INSIGHT

SCRIPTURE 98

SCRIPTURE: (Proverbs 9:10 NKJV)

The fear of the Lord is the beginning of wisdom, and the knowledge of the Holy One is understanding.

DEEPER REFLECTION

There are two things that sincere religion can never fail to attain, one of which is the greatest ingredient, nay, the very foundation of all happiness in this world, and the other of which is the happiness and immortality that await us in the world to come. The latter we can only enjoy now through faith and hope; but the former is present with us, the certain consequence and necessary assistance to a truly virtuous and religious mind. I mean the ease and satisfaction of mind that flow from a proper sense of God and religion, and the rectitude of our desires and intentions to serve him.

A just conception of God, of His excellences and perfections, is the true foundation of religion. Fear is not a voluntary passion. We cannot be afraid or unafraid of things as we please. We fear any being in proportion to the power and will that we conceive that being has to harm or protect us. The different types of fear are not distinguished from each other except by considering the different conceptions or ideas of the things feared. Fear of a tyrant and fear of a father are very different passions; but he who does not know the difference between a tyrant and a father will never be able to distinguish these passions. A just and due fear of God presupposes a right and due conception of God. If men have a wrong idea about God, either as to His holiness and purity, or His justice and mercy, your fear of Him will not produce wisdom. The proposition of the text is equivalent to this: a just notion and conception of God is the beginning of wisdom. We experience in ourselves different types and degrees of fear, which have very different effects and operations. The fear of the Lord is not an abject and servile fear; since God is not a tyrant. The properties of religious fear, as mentioned in the Scriptures, are various. Is it clean? It is hating evil. It is a source of life. There is strong confidence in her. The fear of God means the structure and affection of the soul, which is the consequence of a just notion and conception of the Godhead. It is called the fear of God because, just as majesty and power are the main parts of the idea of God, so fear and reverence are the main ingredients of the affection that springs from it.

The sages of the ancient Near East understood the superiority of wisdom over knowledge, since it encompasses knowledge and also includes moral conduct and understanding. A person was not considered wise, regardless of what knowledge he might have, if his deeds did not conform to his righteous beliefs. Like all the Hebrew intellectual virtues, wisdom... is intensely practical, not theoretical. Basically, wisdom is the art of achieving success, of forming the correct plan to arrive at the desired results. Its seat is the heart, the center of intellectual and moral decision (compare 1 Kings 3:9, 12).

PRAYER

Father, I ask that my children be led by common sense and discernment. May they hang on to them as they would hang on to something of great value. Put something within them that keeps them from having to learn everything the hard way. Instead, let wisdom, common sense, discernment and observation be their teachers. Thank you for enabling them to discover the incredible peace that comes from walking with common sense and discernment. In Jesus' name I pray, AMEN.

FINDING PURPOSE

SCRIPTURE 99

SCRIPTURE: (Jeremiah 29:11 NJKV)

For I know the thoughts that I think toward you, says the Lord, thoughts of peace and not of evil, to give you a future and a hope.

DEEPER REFLECTION

If you are a believer in Jesus Christ, you have a hope and a future that goes far beyond the parameters of this life. If you have a hope and a future where you will live in eternity with God, then this promise that God sets forth in Jeremiah 29:11 is for you. You have the hope "that he who began a good work in you will complete it until the day of Christ Jesus." **(Philippians 1:6)**, and then those who have accepted Jesus as their Savior and made Him Lord of their lives will reign with Christ forever! What great hope we have in the promises of God! This verse from Jeremiah 29:11 tells us that God knows us and has good plans for us, that He is sovereignly directing our lives. His words remind us that God hears our prayers and invites us to seek and know him. In times of uncertainty, this promise is very comforting. We cannot see the future, but this verse gives us encouragement and promises that God has a future and a hope for each of us.

God's plan is not always what we thought it would be. But God's plan is always for the best, even if we don't understand it at the moment. We do know, however, that in all things, God works together for the good of those who love Him. (Romans 8:28) "Furthermore we know that all things work together for good to them that love God, to them who are the called according to his purpose."

We know that when God closes one door, another opens. God is working through every event in our lives to make us more and more dependent on Him for everything we need. We must realize that God's plan is not always the easiest from our point of view, but it is always the best. God sees our future before they become our "today." He sees the beginning of our life, and He sees the end and everything else. (Psalms 139:16) says: "Your eyes saw my embryo, and in your book were written all the days that were given to me, when not one of them existed." God, more than anyone, knows about the plans he has for us.

PRAYER

I know that Your plan for us had existed since before we knew it and that You will fulfill it. Help us to live with a sense of purpose and to understand the calling You have given us. Take away any discouragement we may feel and replace it with the anticipation of what you are doing through us. Help us rest, knowing that your timing is perfect. We pray that nothing will sidetrack us from the plan you have for us. In the name of Jesus, AMEN.

MENTORSHIP

SCRIPTURE 100

SCRIPTURE: (Proverbs 22:6 NKJV)

Train up a child in the way he should go, and when he is old he will not depart from it.

DEEPER REFLECTION

Solomon's advice to parents is, "Train up a child in the way he should go, and when he is old he will not depart from it" (Proverbs 22:6). Raising and training a child within the context of this proverb means that it begins with the Bible, understanding that: "All Scripture is inspired by God, and useful to teach, to reprove, to correct, to instruct..." **(2 Timothy 3:16).** Teaching children the truths of the scriptures will make them wise unto salvation **(2 Timothy 3:15)**; fully equipped for every good work **(2 Timothy 3:17)**; prepared to present a defense with meekness and reverence before everyone who asks them a reason for the hope that is in them **(1 Peter 3:15)**; and prepare them to resist the onslaught of cultures bent on indoctrinating young people with secular values. The Bible tells us that children are a gift from God **(Psalm 127:3).** Surely then, it would seem appropriate to listen to

Solomon's wise advice to form them correctly. In fact, the value that God has placed on teaching our children the truth is clearly addressed by Moses when he emphasized to his people the importance of teaching their children about the Lord, His commandments and laws: "and you shall repeat them to your children, and you shall speak of them when you sit in your house, and when you walk by the way, and when you lie down, and when you rise up. And you shall bind them as a sign on your hand, and they shall be as fronts between your eyes; and you shall write them on the doorposts of your house, and at your gates" **(Deuteronomy 6:7-9).** The Bible clearly teaches that training children to know and obey God is the basis for pleasing Him and living victoriously in His grace. Knowing God and the truths of Him begins with the child's understanding of sin and the need for a Savior. Even very young children understand that they are not perfect and can grasp the need for forgiveness at an early age. Loving parents present a loving God who not only forgives, but offers the perfect sacrifice for sin, and that sacrifice is Jesus Christ. Instructing a child in the way to go means, first of all, directing them to the Savior.

PRAYER

Heavenly Father, thank You for the privilege, responsibility, and joy of the children You have placed in my life. I humbly ask that You would guide me in the way that I should teach them and train them and pray that they may grow up in the fear and nurture of the Lord. May they grow in godly conduct, make wise choices and learn to be both responsible towards others and accountable to authority. Keep them from worldly ways, direct and govern their lives, and may they never depart from the way of righteousness.Father, I pray that my children will experience God's love through the Christian adults and mentors in their lives. In Jesus' name I pray, AMEN.

ALSO BY WILDINE PIERRE

On my way to greatness: Understand the Power of Affirmations, Unlock Your Full Potential and Manifest the Power Within You.

Highly Productive Teens With MAD Social Skills: thrive with friendship, handle peer pressure, bullying, life challenges and everything in between

---

Highly Productive Teens With MAD Devotional Skills: 52 weeks of encouraging devotions and scriptures, to grow your faith, find hope and inspiration, reclaim your identity, and everything in between.